SpringerBriefs in Accounting

Series Editors

SpringerBriefs in Accounting provide a forum for the publication of short books from all areas of accounting, showcasing emerging theory, empirical research, and practical application. They cover a broad range of issues across management accounting, management control, financial and tax accounting, and auditing.

Carlo D'Augusta

Accounting Conservatism and the Stock Market

Insights from Three Decades of Research and New Evidence from the Italian Setting

Springer

Carlo D'Augusta
Bocconi University
Milan, Italy

ISSN 2196-7873 ISSN 2196-7881 (electronic)
SpringerBriefs in Accounting
ISBN 978-3-031-67144-9 ISBN 978-3-031-67145-6 (eBook)
https://doi.org/10.1007/978-3-031-67145-6

This Springer imprint is published by the registered company Springer Nature Switzerland AG
The registered company address is: Gewerbestrasse 11, 6330 Cham, Switzerland

Contents

Chapter 1
Introduction

As the old adage "anticipate no profit, but anticipate all losses" (Bliss, 1924) suggests, prudence and conservatism have long characterized the accounting practice. Evidence of conservatism can be traced to medieval times (Chatfield & Vangermeersch, 1996; Littleton, 1941) and extensive research has shown the pervasiveness of conservatism across various countries and institutional settings, indicating its significance transcends specific markets or periods (Ball et al., 2000; Bushman & Piotroski, 2006). Dating back centuries, conservatism has been recognized as a foundational principle of accounting, which has evolved over time toward increasing conservatism (Watts, 2003).

While conservatism's roots in accounting span centuries, the discourse among scholars and practitioners regarding its desirability is far from new. As noted by Orthaus et al. (2023) in a recent historical review, this "eternal debate" has been shaped by historical contexts, conceptual ambiguities, and divergent assumptions about the purpose of financial reporting. Over time, these debates have evolved in circles, marked by "increasing levels of abstraction" (Orthaus et al., 2023, p. 41). However, by the latter half of the twentieth century, interest in conservatism experienced a notable resurgence, with scholars reinvigorating efforts to understand its role in financial reporting (Basu, 2009).

Pioneering this reawakening of interest, Basu (1997) significantly shaped research on conservatism for subsequent decades. He interpreted conservatism as reflecting asymmetric verification requirements for profits and losses, leading to the faster recognition of bad news compared to good news. This perspective diverged from a different view of conservatism, which focused on implementing accounting methods to minimize net assets' book value and establish off-the-books reserves, which often drew criticism in twentieth-century accounting literature (Orthaus et al., 2023). The theoretical distinction between these two forms of conservatism, later formalized by Beaver and Ryan (2005) as "conditional" and "unconditional" conservatism, injected new life into accounting research. Since then, considerable effort has been dedicated to understanding the determinants and consequences of

C. D'Augusta, *Accounting Conservatism and the Stock Market*, SpringerBriefs in Accounting, https://doi.org/10.1007/978-3-031-67145-6_1

both forms, as well as their connections with other accounting and business phenomena.

In particular, the past 15 years have seen a remarkable surge in research attention toward the relationship between conservatism and the stock market. Two survey papers published in 2010 (Dechow et al., 2010; Armstrong et al., 2010) highlighted the scarcity of studies addressing whether conservatism benefits stock market investors and meets their informational needs. Today, the landscape is vastly different, with intense research activity likely spurred by ongoing debates about the desirability of conservatism in financial reporting.

Indeed, the academic discussion surrounding conservatism has likely been fueled by regulators' increasing opposition, stemming from concerns that conservatism adversely affects the information requirements of the stock market.[1] Understanding the rationale behind this opposition is crucial because conservatism extends beyond mere accounting practices, directly impacting real economic outcomes due to the relevance of accounting numbers for capital providers' decisions. Conservative reporting practices can lead to managerial dismissals, reductions in credit availability, investment downturns, and employee layoffs. Conversely, insufficient conservatism may result in excessive payments to managers or shareholders, depriving the firm of essential resources and potentially causing substantial economic losses for creditors, employees, and other stakeholders.

Given the considerations above, the substantial efforts invested by accounting researchers over the past three decades to explore the economic causes and consequences of conservatism, particularly in relation to capital markets, not only enhance our comprehension of a crucial accounting phenomenon but also of accounting consequences for the real economy. This academic endeavor has tended to focus on the United States despite conservatism's documented prevalence across various institutional and geographical contexts (Ball et al., 2000) and the globalized nature of contemporary financial markets. Notably, the Italian context has witnessed a relative dearth of empirical research addressing fundamental questions tackled by international accounting scholars. Can we observe the effect of capital market forces that demand conservatism in Italy? Do firms respond to such demands by adopting more conservative reporting practices? Do empirical models primarily developed and employed in the U.S. setting effectively capture conservatism when applied to the Italian context? Does conservatism yield positive or adverse informational effects on the Italian stock market? Have such effects surfaced amid the recent unprecedented economic uncertainties and market instabilities triggered by the Covid-19 pandemic?

[1] As observed by Watts (2003), opposition to conservatism often derives from the belief that it provides biased information, thereby hindering the informational needs of external stakeholders, particularly stock market investors seeking accurate valuations. This argument suggests that neutral (i.e., non-conservative) reporting would be more advantageous. Reflecting this sentiment, standard setters in the United States and the European Union have proposed new regulations favoring neutral reporting over conservatism (Kothari et al., 2010).

Since addressing these critical questions requires a comprehensive understanding of the theoretical foundations and empirical approaches employed in conservatism literature, the first part of the book seeks to review the central topics, insights, and contributions advanced by academic researchers over the last three decades. Specifically, Chap. 2 offers an in-depth examination of the historical evolution of conservatism literature's primary theoretical constructs. Subsequently, Chap. 3 reviews the main empirical models employed in this literature to empirically detect manifestations of conservatism and its associations with capital market determinants and outcomes. Following this, Chap. 4 provides a panoramic overview of some of the most influential papers in conservatism literature pertaining to the relationship between conservatism and the stock market.

As the book's first part delves into the foundational theories and empirical frameworks of conservatism literature, the last chapter aims to extend this understanding to the specific context of the Italian stock market. It comprises three distinct empirical studies. The first study explores conservatism within the Italian stock market, emphasizing the need for tailored analyses due to institutional and economic disparities compared to other markets. By exploring various model specifications and capital market pressure drivers, the study extends and validates findings from U.S.-based research to a substantially distinct market environment. The second study examines the role of conservatism in mitigating investor uncertainty during the Covid-19 crisis in the Italian stock market. Through an analysis of pre- and post-lockdown periods, this study shows the significant impact of firms' conservatism levels on stock market outcomes, contributing to our understanding of the Italian stock market dynamics during crises. Lastly, the third study investigates shifts in conservatism among Italian firms as they were recovering from the pandemic, shedding light on managerial incentives and capital market pressures as pivotal influencers of reporting behavior. Thus, the study underscores the importance of understanding how economic crises affect reporting conservatism across diverse contexts.

References

Armstrong, C. S., Guay, W. R., & Weber, J. P. (2010). The role of information and financial reporting in corporate governance and debt contracting. *Journal of Accounting and Economics, 50*(2–3), 179–234.

Ball, R., Kothari, S. P., & Robin, A. (2000). The effect of international institutional factors on properties of accounting earnings. *Journal of Accounting and Economics, 29*, 1–51.

Basu, S. (1997). The conservatism principle and the asymmetric timeliness of earnings. *Journal of Accounting and Economics, 24*(1), 3–37.

Basu, S. (2009). Conservatism research: Historical development and future prospects. *China Journal of Accounting Research, 2*(1), 1–20.

Beaver, W. H., & Ryan, S. G. (2005). Conditional and unconditional conservatism: Concepts and modeling. *Review of Accounting Studies, 10*(2–3), 269–309.

Bliss, J. H. (1924). *Management through accounts* (2nd ed.). The Ronald Press. http://scholar.google.com/scholar?hl=en&btnG=Search&q=intitle:Management+through+Accounts#0

Bushman, R. M., & Piotroski, J. D. (2006). Financial reporting incentives for conservative accounting: The influence of legal and political institutions. *Journal of Accounting and Economics, 42*(1–2), 107–148.
Chatfield, M., & Vangermeersch, R. (1996). *History of accounting: An international encyclopedia.* Individual and Corporate Publications. https://egrove.olemiss.edu/acct_corp/168
Dechow, P. M., Ge, W., & Schrand, C. M. (2010). Understanding earnings quality: A review of the proxies, their determinants and their consequences. *Journal of Accounting and Economics, 50*, 344–401.
Kothari, S. P., Ramanna, K., & Skinner, D. J. (2010). Implications for GAAP from an analysis of positive research in accounting. *Journal of Accounting and Economics, 50*, 246–286.
Littleton, A. C. (1941). A genealogy for «cost or market». *Accounting Review, 16*(2), 161.
Orthaus, S., Pelger, C., & Kuhner, C. (2023). The eternal debate over conservatism and prudence: A historical perspective on the conceptualization of asymmetry in financial accounting theory*. *Contemporary Accounting Research, 40*(1), 41–88.
Watts, R. L. (2003). Conservatism in accounting part I: Explanations and implications. *Accounting Horizons, 17*(3), 207–221.

Chapter 2
Conceptual Developments

2.1 Historical Perspectives on Conservatism

Conservatism is one of the enduring pillars of financial accounting, a notion widely acknowledged throughout the accounting literature. According to Sterling (1967, p. 110), it is “the most ancient and probably the most pervasive principle of accounting valuation.” Accounting historians have uncovered evidence supporting the early adoption of what are now recognized as conditionally conservative accounting practices. For instance, findings by Littleton (1941) and Basu (2009) shed light on asset valuation practices dating back to as early as 1412, where assets were recorded at the lower of cost or market value. In particular, vineyards and other assets were subject to write-downs exceeding 30% of historical cost due to impairments, while utensils and furniture faced similar treatment as appraisers deemed their values to have deteriorated. Further insights from Chatfield and Vangermeersch (1996) reveal the regular practice among Florentine bankers of adjusting accounts receivable to their net realizable value. Moreover, the first printed book on accounting for non-profit organizations in the sixteenth century[1] recommended the prudent writing down of certain assets and goods to prevent their valuation from exceeding market prices upon sale (Chatfield & Vangermeersch, 1996). Additionally, Penndorf (1930) illustrated how medieval Italian businessmen were incentivized by tax benefits to employ accounting practices to minimize the net value of business assets, a practice akin to what is now considered as tax-driven unconditional conservatism.

Chatfield and Vangermeersch (1996, p. 160) asserted that conservatism in contemporary accounting practices traces its origins to medieval stewardship accounting. They highlighted that “concealment of unrealized gains was the steward’s

[1] Pietra, Angelo, (1586). *“Indrizzo de gli economi, o sia Ordinatissima instruttione da regolatamente formare qualunque scrittura in un libro doppio ... ”*. Individual and Corporate Publications. 4. https://egrove.olemiss.edu/acct_corp/4

C. D’Augusta, *Accounting Conservatism and the Stock Market*, SpringerBriefs in Accounting, https://doi.org/10.1007/978-3-031-67145-6_2

natural response to the feudal stipulation that the lord must suffer no loss from fraud, negligence, or bad judgment." Their argument underscores how historical economic incentives made it safer to understate net assets. This perspective resonates with recent theoretical and empirical research suggesting that conservatism arises in response to agency conflicts between firms and contracting parties and the litigation risk arising from such conflicts. Furthermore, in their discussion of the evolution of accounting practices during the 1800s, Chatfield and Vangermeersch (1996, p. 96) proposed that "an accounting policy of systematic understatement seemed a natural antidote to management's known tendency to overstate," noting that conservatism's "early advocates were creditors who wished to protect paid-in capital against excessive dividend payments."

During the late nineteenth to early twentieth century, the discourse among accounting scholars and practitioners predominantly depicted conservatism as an approach leading to understating net assets, often resulting in hidden reserves, in line with the notion that financial reporting primarily served to aid banks' lending decisions. However, by the early 1900s, as pre-classical theory emerged and attention shifted toward accounting as an information source for capital market participants, such practices began to face criticism (Orthaus et al., 2023). A recurring critique centered on the belief that a conservative bias in asset valuation could have adverse implications for stock market investors.

For instance, Hatfield (1922, p. 108) discussed how conservatism prevents the recognition of internally generated goodwill. He characterized this approach as prudent, albeit possibly illogical, yet deemed it necessary "to prevent a harmful exaggeration [because] human nature is so incurably optimistic, especially when estimating one's own possessions." However, Hatfield (1922) cautioned against the understatement of net assets and the resultant creation of hidden reserves, suggesting that it "may be used as a means of refusing to pay dividends" or "it may lead ignorant stockholders [...] to dispose of their stock" (Hatfield, 1922, p. 254). Similarly, Scott et al. (1926, p. 19) adopted a critical stance toward the purported advantages of conservatism. They contended that "an intentional understatement of asset values will aggravate rather than counteract any tendency of business management to be overoptimistic." In a parallel vein, Daniels (1934) alerted to the potential misuse of conservative asset write-downs by managers aiming to deceive investors by manipulating future income statements via reduced depreciation expenses.

Criticism of conservatism surged notably in the post-war era, coinciding with the ascendance of decision-usefulness for capital market allocation decisions as the prevailing paradigm for standard setting (Orthaus et al., 2023). Devine (1963, p. 127) observed that "avant-garde accountants in America [think that] conservatism is not a defense for anything and therefore is not a positive force in argument" underscoring that earnings understatements can lead to inefficient decision-making by investors, as they "excite existing owners to sell, and [...] prospective buyers to refrain from buying" (Devine, 1963, p. 129). Furthermore, in 1980, the Financial Accounting

Standards Board's Statement of Financial Accounting Concept No. 2 explicitly addressed conservatism, highlighting that it introduces a downward bias in financial reporting which "conflicts with significant qualitative characteristics, such as representational faithfulness, neutrality, and comparability" (para. 92).

While a comprehensive exploration of the historical evolution of conservatism and the debate surrounding its desirability lies beyond this book's scope, the overview above underscores two enduring themes in discussions about conservatism and its implications for stock market investors. Firstly, there appears to be no universally agreed-upon conceptual definition of conservatism. Instead, practitioners and academics often characterized it as involving persistent understatement of asset values, intentional bias in reported earnings for a given period, creation of hidden reserves, or application of lower of cost or market rules. Secondly, in the latter decades of the twentieth century, regulators, practitioners, and academics increasingly voiced concerns about conservatism's adverse information effects on the valuation requirements of stock market investors. Allegedly, these investors favor a financial accounting system characterized by unbiased information that is reported neutrally rather than the conservatism that is often perceived as distorting such information.

In the mid-nineties, a resurgence of interest emerged among academics seeking to reexamine conservatism and its connection to valuation and the informational needs of the stock market. According to Basu (2009), this renewed interest in conservatism research can be traced to a call made at the 1993 annual American Accounting Association meeting to delve into the reasons behind the conservative bias in financial reporting. A pivotal paper marking the onset of this new wave of conservatism research, central to the focus of this book, is undoubtedly Basu (1997). In this work, Basu reconceptualized conservatism, defining it as "capturing accountants' tendency to require a higher degree of verification for recognizing good news than bad news in financial statements" (Basu, 1997, p.4). This difference in verification requirements between profits and losses leads to the asymmetric timeliness of their recognition, which in turn influences specific empirical aspects such as "the association between earnings and returns or the time series of earnings changes" (Basu, 1997, p.4). The impact of Basu's (1997) conservatism model was profound, both theoretically and empirically, catalyzing over two decades of scientific inquiry that shed fresh insights on the relationship between conservatism and the stock market, the central focus of this book.

After the publication of Basu (1997), there arose a need within the literature to distinguish between various forms of conservatism and analyze their distinct empirical characteristics, consequences, and antecedents. As elaborated in the following sections, these distinctions constitute a fundamental component of the theoretical foundations underlying much of the subsequent empirical research on conservatism and its relationship with the stock market.

2.2 Modern Perspectives

2.2.1 Conditional vs. Unconditional Conservatism

Following Basu's seminal contribution in 1997, there was a surge of literature exploring the concept of conservatism and dissecting its empirical implications. This body of work began to propose the existence of two distinct forms. However, because "the literature [was] very recent, the terminology [was] inconsistent across studies" (Pae et al., 2005, p. 697). For instance, Pae et al. (2005) referred to such distinction as ex ante vs. ex post conservatism, and Chandra et al. (2004) labeled the two forms as news-independent and news-dependent conservatism.

In a highly influential paper that would shape subsequent research significantly, Beaver and Ryan (2005, p. 269) defined conservatism as "the on average understatement of the book value of net assets relative to their market value." They presented a model illustrating the distinct characteristics and interactions between two forms of conservatism, which they categorized as "unconditional" and "conditional." Under the former form, corresponding to what other studies had termed "news-independent" or "ex-ante," the average understatement of net assets stems from aspects of the accounting process that generate unrecorded goodwill. These aspects are determined at the inception of assets and liabilities and remain unaffected by subsequent information arrivals concerning the expected future cash flows derived from the asset or liability.

Consider, for instance, a scenario where a firm acquires a long-term productive asset like property, plant, and equipment. In the initial year of usage, the firm must select a depreciation method to systematically reduce the asset's net book value and allocate its cost over the asset's productive life. Opting for an accelerated depreciation method over a straight-line depreciation will lead to earlier recognition of expenses, resulting in a lower average value of net assets, while the asset's revenue-generating performance remains constant. However, this reduction in net assets arises solely from a pre-determined choice (i.e., accelerated vs. straight-line depreciation) made at the asset's inception, independent of subsequent economic developments regarding the asset. Consequently, the firm will not alter its depreciation method based on later information about the asset's cash generation. Therefore, net assets in subsequent periods reflect the unconditional effect of the firm's decision to adopt an accelerated depreciation method. Similar instances of unconditional conservatism include selecting last-in first-out assumptions for determining ending inventory values and the cost of goods sold, or deciding whether to expense or capitalize certain costs.

In contrast to unconditional conservatism, which remains unaffected by post-inception economic events impacting assets and liabilities, the second form of conservatism is "conditional" on the nature and magnitude of those events. Beaver and Ryan (2005) define this conditional form of conservatism as the practice of writing down the book value of assets under sufficiently adverse circumstances but not writing it up under favorable circumstances. To illustrate, consider the previous example: if adverse events worsen the company's expectations regarding the long-term asset's revenue-generating capacity to a significant extent, the company will recognize an impairment loss, reducing the asset's net book value. However, suppose expectations improve (i.e., the asset's cash flows are anticipated to exceed the original estimates). In that case, the company will not immediately recognize any gain or increase in net assets, allowing the economic impact to manifest gradually in the financial statements as the positive event unfolds. Thus, this form of conservatism is contingent upon economic conditions deteriorating beyond a certain threshold, with write-down losses being recognized in such instances, whereas improving economic conditions never trigger the recognition of write-up gains. An example of conditional conservatism is the recognition of impairment losses when an asset's net book value exceeds its expected future cash flows. Another example is the increase in the cost of goods sold when inventory's net realizable value falls below its carrying value. Beaver and Ryan's (2005) definition of conditional conservatism aligns with Basu's (1997) interpretation as an asymmetry in verification requirements that leads to an asymmetry in recognition timeliness. Basu's definition has since become a standard reference for conditional conservatism in the literature.

Beaver and Ryan (2005) asserted that the two forms of conservatism are not independent but interact, yielding significant implications. Unconditional conservatism plays a pivotal role in generating unrecorded goodwill as it consistently leads to the understatement of net assets. Referring to the previous example, the adoption of accelerated depreciation methods or Last-In First-Out (LIFO) valuation assumptions consistently undervalues long-term assets and inventory relative to their true economic worth. This creation of accounting slack hinders the subsequent application of conditional conservatism. For instance, when an inventory's carrying value has been kept artificially low since its inception, it is less likely for its net realizable value to fall below this reduced carrying value. Similarly, even a substantial decline in future cash flows may fail to trigger an impairment if the asset's net book value has already been driven close to its lower limit due to years of accelerated depreciation. Thus, unconditional conservatism precludes the emergence of future conditional conservatism. Conversely, conditional conservatism adjusts the cost basis of assets, thereby influencing subsequent instances of unconditional conservatism.

Ball and Shivakumar (2005, p. 90) asserted that understanding the distinction between conditional and unconditional conservatism is crucial for grasping how conservatism can facilitate efficient contracting within firms. They contended that "it is difficult to see how contracting is affected by conservatism in the form of an unconditional accounting bias of known magnitude. Rational agents would simply invert the bias. [...] Further, an unconditional bias of unknown magnitude introduces randomness in decisions based on financial information and can only reduce contracting efficiency." While they regarded unconditional conservatism as inefficient or, at best, neutral in contracting, they argued that the conditional form could offer contracting benefits by ensuring timelier recognition of economic losses. This asymmetric timeliness could, for example, aid in debt contracting by hastening debt covenant violations or diminish managers' incentives to pursue value-decreasing investments. Therefore, Ball and Shivakumar's (2005) arguments emphasize that conditional and unconditional conservatism are substantially different concepts from a contracting perspective.

Qiang (2007) offered further insights into the disparities between conditional and unconditional conservatism, particularly regarding their implications for contracting. Aligned with Basu's (1997) interpretation, Qiang (2007, p. 760) contended that conditional conservatism "requires a higher degree of verification for good news than for bad news after difficult-to-verify news occurs." In contrast, unconditional conservatism "also addresses difficult-to-verify information and biases the numbers downward; however, this form is applied before difficult-to-verify news occurs." Thus, as noted by Beaver and Ryan (2005), unconditional conservatism immunizes accounting systems against future bad news. Expanding on this concept, Qiang (2007) underscored the possibility of a trade-off between the two forms; hence, economic factors that enhance one form of conservatism may exert opposing effects on the other. Consistent with this notion, Qiang (2007) finds that firms facing higher equity and debt contracting costs tend to adopt greater conditional conservatism. However, elevated litigation costs contribute to increased conservatism in both forms, while regulation costs prompt firms to embrace greater unconditional conservatism. Additionally, tax considerations prompt firms to lean toward unconditional conservatism.

The two forms of conservatism can exhibit significant differences in their valuation implications. In this context, Chen et al. (2014) argued that faster recognition of loss events compared to gain events results in a smaller persistence of accounting losses and a higher persistence of profits. Moreover, Chen et al. (2014, p. 234) contended that "if firms overestimate the financial impact of bad news events in efforts to report conservatively, the reversals of these negative accruals will likely be recognized gradually through time in future periods, which may also increase the persistence of future earnings." Since earnings persistence estimates are crucial for valuation purposes, these properties of conservatism are likely to have implications for valuation. Consistent with this proposition, Chen et al. (2014) showed that conditional conservatism renders earnings less persistent than unconditional conservatism, and the pricing multiple on earnings is smaller for the former form.

To summarize, significant research has been devoted to unraveling the stock market impacts of conditional and unconditional conservatism in recent decades. Some studies have delved into one form exclusively, while others have examined both. As outlined in Chap. 4, many of these studies have utilized diverse empirical methods to gauge these types of conservatism. While a thorough discussion of conservatism's empirical measurement will be elaborated in Chap. 3, Table 2.1 showcases a selection of notable papers that have explored either or both forms and the empirical frameworks they have employed.

Table 2.1 Selection of prominent studies analyzing either or both forms of conservatism and the primary empirical models they adopt to measure conservatism

Authors & year	Journal	Form	Main empirical models employed to measure conservatism
Kim and Pevzner (2010)	JAPP	Conditional	Asymmetric earnings-returns association (Basu, 1997); Asymmetric earnings changes' persistence (Basu, 1997); Asymmetric accrual-cash flow association (Ball & Shivakumar, 2005); Earnings skewness (Givoly & Hayn, 2000); Cumulative negative accruals (Givoly & Hayn, 2000).
D'Augusta and DeAngelis (2020)	CAR	Conditional	Asymmetric earnings-returns association (Khan & Watts, 2009); Earnings skewness (Givoly & Hayn, 2000); Conservatism's ratio (Callen et al., 2010).
Garcìa Lara et al. (2011)	RAST	Conditional	Conservatism's ratio (Callen et al. 2010)
LaFond and Watts (2008)	TAR	Conditional	Asymmetric earnings-returns association (Basu, 1997)
Kim et al. (2013)	TAR	Conditional	Asymmetric earnings-returns association (Khan & Watts, 2009); Earnings skewness (Givoly & Hayn, 2000); Cumulative negative accruals (Givoly & Hayn, 2000).
Hui et al. (2009)	JAE	Unconditional	Hidden reserves (Penman & Zhang, 2002); Cumulative negative accruals (Givoly & Hayn, 2000); M/B ratio bias (Beaver & Ryan, 2005)
Kim et al. (2019)	CAR	Unconditional	Hidden reserves (Penman & Zhang, 2002)
Jaggi et al. (2021)	JAAF	Unconditional	Hidden reserves (Penman & Zhang, 2002); Cumulative negative accruals (Givoly & Hayn, 2000); M/B ratio bias (Beaver & Ryan, 2005)
Mensah et al. (2004)	JAAF	Unconditional	Hidden reserves (Penman & Zhang, 2002); Cumulative negative accruals (Givoly & Hayn, 2000)
Mashruwala and Mashruwala (2018)	CAR	Both	Hidden reserves (Penman & Zhang, 2002); Cumulative negative accruals (Givoly & Hayn, 2000)
Biddle et al. (2022)	JAAF	Both	Hidden reserves (Penman & Zhang, 2002); Cumulative negative accruals (Givoly & Hayn, 2000); M/B ratio bias (Beaver & Ryan, 2005); Asymmetric earnings-returns association (Khan & Watts, 2009); Conservatism's ratio (Callen et al. 2010).
Cano-Rodríguez (2010)	EAR	Both	Asymmetric accrual-cash flow association (Ball & Shivakumar, 2005)
Chen et al. (2014)	EAR	Both	Cumulative negative accruals (Givoly & Hayn, 2000); Earnings skewness (Givoly & Hayn, 2000);
Francis et al. (2013)	AH	Both	Asymmetric earnings-returns association (Basu, 1997; Khan & Watts, 2009); Earnings skewness (Givoly & Hayn, 2000); M/B ratio bias (Beaver & Ryan, 2005)
Qiang (2007)	TAR	Both	Asymmetric B/M ratio-returns association (Beaver & Ryan, 2005)

2.2.2 Balance Sheet Vs. Income Statement Conservatism

In addition to the dichotomy between conditional and unconditional conservatism, another distinction emerged in the literature, focusing on the financial statement impacted by conservatism. Due to the characteristics of the double-entry system, conservatism yields two primary effects. On the balance sheet, it leads to the understatement of accumulated net assets due to the higher valuation of liabilities and the lower valuation of assets, respectively. This effect is often referred to as "balance sheet conservatism" (Sunder et al., 2018). Conversely, on the income statement, conservatism results in lower current earnings owing to the accelerated recognition of economic losses and the delayed recognition of profits.

Balance sheet conservatism represents a stable manifestation of conservatism arising from the cumulative effects of conservative accounting practices in preceding periods (Sunder et al., 2018). In contrast, earnings conservatism is more transient. As noted by Weil et al. (2012, p. 754), "over long-enough time spans, income is cash-in less cash-out. If a (conservative) reporting method shows less income in early periods, it must show higher income in some later period." Similarly, D'Augusta and Redigolo (2019, p. 433) argued that "higher conservatism in the current year's income statement will reduce current earnings because of the faster recognition of expenses and losses and/or the deferral of uncertain profits. However, it will also increase future earnings when the recognition of the deferred profits eventually begins, and the recognition of expenses and losses stops or declines."

Earlier literature has occasionally utilized the terms "balance sheet" and "income statement" conservatism to denote the contrast between the conditional and unconditional forms of conservatism (Ball et al., 2000; García Lara & Mora, 2004). However, as highlighted by Beaver and Ryan (2005, p. 305), associating the two forms of conservatism with a dichotomy of balance sheet versus income statement might be misleading because both forms "affect the income statement and balance sheet consistently if the clean surplus relation holds and transactions in the firm's equity are accounted for at fair value." Watts (2003, p. 208) echoed Beaver and Ryan (2005), cautioning that conditional conservatism is not the antithesis of balance sheet conservatism, noting that "an important consequence of conservatism's asymmetric treatment of gains and losses is the persistent understatement of net asset values." Similarly, Sunder et al. (2018, p. 496) contended that "balance sheet conservatism arises from past conservatism in earnings, both conditional and unconditional." In line with this argument, they examine the impact of balance sheet conservatism on borrowing costs and discover that lenders value balance sheet conservatism stemming from conditional, but not unconditional, conservatism in earnings.

Confusion between the two distinctions, namely balance sheet versus income statement and unconditional versus conditional, may arise partly due to their similar negative interrelationship. Indeed, similar to conditional and unconditional conservatism, higher balance sheet conservatism can lead to less conservatism in future income statements. Liabilities cannot infinitely increase, and assets cannot be written below the expected salvage value. Therefore, the greater the balance sheet conservatism, the more conservative charges accumulate in prior years' earnings, reducing the likelihood of such conservative charges persisting. This negative association has sometimes provided regulators with grounds to oppose conservatism in accounting. For example, The Accounting Research Bulletin (ARB) 2 (AICPA, 1939) suggests that "conservatism in the balance sheet is of dubious value if attained at the expense of conservatism in the income statement, which is far more significant." Addressing this concern, Watts (2003, p. 208) argued against the notion that conservatism is confined to a specific period's income statement effect, as suggested by conservatism critics; rather, it encompasses the "cumulative financial effects represented in the balance sheet and to income or earnings cumulated since the firm began operation."

2.2.3 *Discretionary vs. Non-discretionary Conservatism*

Lawrence et al. (2013) introduced a third distinction, highlighting that conservatism is a prevalent feature of accounting regulation. For instance, Generally Accepted Accounting Principles (GAAP) mandate the write-down of non-financial assets if their fair value drops below the carrying amount but prohibit companies from writing assets up in case of the opposite scenario. Therefore, firms' practice of not increasing assets' book value above historical cost is not a conservative choice but rather a reflection of their adherence to conservative accounting standards. Expanding on this notion, Lawrence et al. (2013) differentiated between two alternative forms of conservatism: non-discretionary and discretionary. They define the former as conservatism mandated by accounting rules and the latter as conservatism "arising from purposeful intervention in the financial reporting process to adjust the amount and timing of conservative accounting" (Lawrence et al., 2013, p. 113).

Lawrence et al. (2013) argued that the differentiation between discretionary and non-discretionary conservatism is significant because some explanations proposed in the literature for the observed variability in conservatism may align with the former but not the latter. For example, they noted that certain findings linking conservatism to efficient contracting seem to be explained by non-discretionary conservatism. However, Lawrence et al. (2013) also demonstrated that non-discretionary conservatism accounts for only a small portion of the documented variability in conservatism, indicating a significant degree of discretion in firms' application of conservative accounting practices. Indeed, Roychowdhury and Martin (2013, p. 135) remarked, based on Lawrence et al. (2013), that "even within the largely rules-based approach towards financial standards inherent in U.S. GAAP, managers often enjoy substantial discretion in accounting choice. [...] Empirical patterns in the data generally point to managers enjoying substantial discretion in determining the timing and magnitude of asset write-downs." Moreover, empirical evidence presented by Collins et al. (2024) and Ahmed and Duellman (2013) indicates that conservatism correlates with managers' behavioral traits, such as optimistic sentiment and overconfidence, underscoring the discretionary nature of the variability in conservatism across firms.

References

Ahmed, A. S., & Duellman, S. (2013). Managerial overconfidence and accounting conservatism. *Journal of Accounting Research, 51*(1), 1–30.

American Institute of Certified Public Accountants (AICPA), Committee on Accounting Procedures. 1939. Unamortized Discount and Redemption Premium on Bonds Refunded. Accounting Research Bulletin, No. 2. AICPA.

Ball, R., Kothari, S. P., & Robin, A. (2000). The effect of international institutional factors on properties of accounting earnings. *Journal of Accounting and Economics, 29*, 1–51.

Ball, R., & Shivakumar, L. (2005). Earnings quality in UK private firms: Comparative loss recognition timeliness. *Journal of Accounting and Economics, 39*(1), 83–128.

Basu, S. (1997). The conservatism principle and the asymmetric timeliness of earnings. *Journal of Accountingand Economics, 24*(1), 3–37.

Basu, S. (2009). Conservatism research: Historical development and future prospects. *China Journal of Accounting Research, 2*(1), 1–20.

Beaver, W. H., & Ryan, S. G. (2005). Conditional and unconditional conservatism: Concepts and modeling. *Review of Accounting Studies, 10*(2–3), 269–309.

Biddle, G. C., Ma, M. L. Z., & Song, F. M. (2022). Accounting Conservatism and Bankruptcy Risk. *Journal ofAccounting, Auditing & Finance, 37*(2), 295–323.

Callen, J. L., Segal, D., & Hope, O.-K. (2010). The pricing of conservative accounting and the measurement ofconservatism at the firm-year level. *Review of Accounting Studies, 15*(1), 145–178.

Cano-Rodríguez, M. (2010). Big Auditors, Private Firms and Accounting Conservatism: Spanish Evidence.*European Accounting Review, 19*(1), 131–159.

Chandra, U., Wasley, C. E., & Waymire, G. B. (2004). Income conservatism in the U.S. technology sector. Available at SSRN 485064.

Chatfield, M., & Vangermeersch, R. (1996). *History of accounting: An international encyclopedia*. Individual and Corporate Publications. https://egrove.olemiss.edu/acct_corp/168

Chen, L. H., Folsom, D., Paek, W., & Sami, H. (2014). Accounting conservatism, earnings persistence and pricing multiples on earnings. *Accounting Horizons, 28*(2), 233–260.

Collins, D. W., Nguyen, N. Q., & Nguyen, T. T. (2024). Manager sentiment and conditional conservatism. *Journal of Business Finance & Accounting*.

D'Augusta, C., & DeAngelis, M. D. (2020). Does accounting conservatism discipline qualitative disclosure? Evidence from tone management in the MD&A. *Contemporary Accounting Research, 37*(4), 2287–2318.

D'Augusta, C., & Redigolo, G. (2019). Do firms use early guidance to disclose the effect of conservatism on future earnings? *Review of Accounting and Finance, 18*(3), 432–455.

Daniels, M. B. (1934). Principles of asset valuation. *Accounting Review, 9*(2), 114.

Devine, C. (1963). The rule of conservatism reexamined. *Journal of Accounting Research, 1*(2), 127–138.

Francis, B., Hasan, I., & Wu, Q. (2013). The benefits of conservative accounting to shareholders: Evidence fromthe financial crisis. *Accounting Horizons, 27*(2), 319–349.

García Lara, J. M., & Mora, A. (2004). Balance sheet versus earnings conservatism in Europe. *European Accounting Review, 13*(2), 261–292.

García, J. M., Garcìa Osma, B., & Penalva, F. (2011). Conditional conservatism and cost of capital.*Review of Accounting Studies, 16*(2), 247–271.

Givoly, D., & Hayn, C. (2000). The changing time-series properties of earnings, cash flows and accruals: Hasfinancial reporting become more conservative? *Journal of Accounting and Economics, 29*(3), 287–320.

Hatfield, H. R. (1922). *Modern accounting: Its principles and some of its problems*. Appleton. http://archive.org/details/modernaccounting00hatfuoft

Hui, K. W., Matsunaga, S. R., & Morse, D. (2009). The impact of conservatism on management earningsforecasts. *Journal of Accounting and Economics, 47*(3), 192–207.

Jaggi, B., Ronen, J., & Xin, H. (2021). Management Earnings Forecast and Accounting Conservatism. *JournalofAccounting, Auditing & Finance, 36*(3), 451–474.

Khan, M., & Watts, R. L. (2009). Estimation and empirical properties of a firm-year measure of accountingconservatism. *Journal of Accounting and Economics, 48*(2–3), 132–150.

Kim, B. H., & Pevzner, M. (2010). Conditional accounting conservatism and future negative surprises: Anempirical investigation. *Journal of Accounting and Public Policy, 29*(4), 311–329.

Kim, Y., Li, S., Pan, C., & Zuo, L. (2013). The Role of Accounting Conservatism in the Equity Market: Evidencefrom Seasoned Equity Offerings. *The Accounting Review, 88*(4), 1327–1356.

Kim, J. B., Nekrasov, A., Shroff, P. K., & Simon, A. (2019). Valuation Implications of Unconditional AccountingConservatism: Evidence from Analysts' Target Prices. *Contemporary Accounting Research, 36*(3), 1669–1698.

LaFond, R., & Watts, R. L. (2008). The Information Role of Conservatism. *The Accounting Review, 83*(2), 447–478.

Lawrence, A., Sloan, R., & Sun, Y. (2013). Non-discretionary conservatism: Evidence and implications. *Journal of Accounting & Economics, 56*, 112–133.

Littleton, A. C. (1941). A genealogy for «cost or market». *Accounting Review, 16*(2), 161.

Mashruwala, C., & Mashruwala, S. (2018). Does Accounting Conservatism Reduce Overpricing Caused byShort-Sales Constraints? *Contemporary Accounting Research, 35*(4), 2160–2190.

Mensah, Y. M., Song, X., & Ho, S. S. M. (2004). The Effect of Conservatism on Analysts' Annual EarningsForecast Accuracy and Dispersion. *Journal of Accounting, Auditing & Finance, 19*(2), 159–183.

Orthaus, S., Pelger, C., & Kuhner, C. (2023). The eternal debate over conservatism and prudence: A historical perspective on the conceptualization of asymmetry in financial accounting theory*. *Contemporary Accounting Research, 40*(1), 41–88.

Pae, J., Thornton, D. B., & Welker, M. (2005). The link between earnings conservatism and the price to book ratio. *Contemporary Accounting Research, 22*(3), 693–717.

Penman, S. H., & Zhang, X.-J. (2002). Accounting conservatism, the quality of earnings, and stock returns. *TheAccounting Review, 77*(2), 237–264.

Penndorf, B. (1930). The relation of taxation to the history of the balance sheet. *The Accounting Review, 5*(3), 243–251.

Qiang, X. (2007). The effects of contracting, litigation, regulation, and tax costs on conditional and unconditional conservatism: Cross-sectional evidence at the firm level. *The Accounting Review, 82*(3), 759–796.

Roychowdhury, S., & Martin, X. (2013). Understanding discretion in conservatism: An alternative viewpoint. *Journal of Accounting & Economics, 56*, 134–146.

Scott, D., Jackson, J. H., Filbey, E. J., Reighard, J. J., Rittenhouse, C. F., & Paton, W. A. (1926). Conservatism in inventory valuations. *The Accounting Review, 1*(1), 18–30.

Sterling, R. R. (1967). Conservatism: The fundamental principle of valuation in traditional accounting*. *Abacus, 3*(2), 109–132.

Sunder, J., Sunder, S. V., & Zhang, J. (2018). Balance sheet conservatism and debt contracting. *Contemporary Accounting Research, 35*(1), 494–524.

Watts, R. L. (2003). Conservatism in accounting part I: Explanations and implications. *Accounting Horizons, 17*(3), 207–221.

Weil, R. L., Schipper, K., & Francis, J. (2012). *Financial accounting: An introduction to concepts, methods and uses* (14th ed.). South-Western College Pub.

Chapter 3
Measurement of Conservatism for Empirical Research

3.1 Conditional Conservatism: Basu (1997)

As discussed in Chap. 2, Basu (1997, p. 3) interpreted conservatism as "capturing accountants' tendency to require a higher degree of verification for recognizing good news than bad news in financial statements." Basu's (1997) interpretation of the conservatism principle has profoundly impacted accounting literature, which has often adopted it as the definition of conditional conservatism.[1] Indeed, Basu (1997) is credited with significantly contributing to the beginning of the stream of empirical research on conditional conservatism (Beaver & Ryan, 2005).[2] Under this interpretation of conservatism, good news is reflected in earnings more slowly than bad news. As Watts (2003, p. 208) noted, "this interpretation allows for degrees of conservatism: the greater the difference in the degree of verification required for gains versus losses, the greater the conservatism." In other words, by measuring the magnitude of such difference, it is possible to obtain a measure of the degree of conservatism that characterizes a group of firms; in addition, by testing whether such difference is larger for some firms than for others, it is possible to estimate whether variations in the degree of conservatism are associated with other variables. In this way, the Basu (1997) study provided the literature with a new theoretical perspective on conservatism and a model that could be used to measure it for hypothesis testing.

In particular, Basu (1997) identified two asymmetries that stem from firms' application of conditionally conservative accounting: (1) the asymmetry in the timeliness of the recognition of news into earnings and (2) the asymmetry in the

[1] Consider, for instance, Ball et al. (2000, 2008), Chen, Chen, and Cheng (2014), Lee et al. (2015), Liu and Elayan (2015), Pae et al. (2005), Watts (2003).

[2] Beaver and Ryan (2005, p. 301): "Research on conditional conservatism is more recent and empirical than research on unconditional conservatism, beginning with Basu (1995, 1997), and in our view merits considerable further attention by accounting researchers."

C. D'Augusta, *Accounting Conservatism and the Stock Market*, SpringerBriefs in Accounting, https://doi.org/10.1007/978-3-031-67145-6_3

persistence of such earnings. The intuition behind the existence of these asymmetries is as follows. If the accounting system recognizes bad news quickly but waits before recognizing good news until higher verification requirements have been met, then earnings will be more strongly associated with concurrent publicly available economic news when the latter is negative; vice versa, the association of good news with current earnings will be weaker as such news is incorporated into earnings gradually over time. Consequently, the association between current earnings and economic news will be asymmetric—specifically, it will be steeper for bad news than good news. Moreover, the association between current and future earnings will also be asymmetric. Specifically, profits will be more likely to continue and losses more likely to revert because the former are usually spread over multiple periods, while the latter are typically recognized immediately in their entirety.

Based on Basu's (1997) model, the magnitude of the first asymmetry can be empirically assessed by measuring economic news using unexpected stock market returns. This approach involves testing whether the slope of a regression of current earnings (EARN) on current market returns (RET) is steeper when RET is negative than positive. Thus, the following regression equation can be expressed:

$$\text{EARN} = \beta 0 + \beta 1\text{RET} + \beta 2\text{NEG} + \beta 3\text{RET} * \text{NEG} + \varepsilon, \quad (3.1)$$

In the equation above, EARN represents net income before extraordinary items scaled by the market value of equity at the beginning of the year, while RET denotes the stock market return over the year.[3] Additionally, NEG is a binary variable identifying observations characterized by negative returns; specifically, NEG equals 1 when RET is negative and 0 otherwise. The coefficient β1 reflects the average responsiveness of recognized earnings to concurrent good news: a higher β1 indicates that observations in the sample tend to incorporate publicly available good news into earnings more promptly, thus recognizing profits faster. Furthermore, the sum of coefficients β1 and β3 represents the average responsiveness of recognized earnings to concurrent bad news. A higher sum indicates that observations in the sample recognize losses faster in response to publicly available bad news. The coefficient β3 represents the asymmetry in the timeliness of recognizing good and bad news: a more positive β3 indicates that bad news is recognized more promptly than good news, reflecting higher conditional conservatism.

To empirically measure the magnitude of the second asymmetry, the model can be modified using the current year-over-year change in earnings (ΔE) as the independent variable and the future change (ΔE(t + 1)) as the dependent variable. The equation is then formulated as follows:

[3] In alternative specifications of the model, Basu (1997), as well as subsequent studies by other researchers, has measured RET using: (1) market-adjusted returns vs. simple returns, (2) buy-and-hold returns vs. cumulative returns, (3) returns computed over the fiscal year vs. over the period between two earnings announcements. The validity of the model, as well as the inference that can be gained by using the model to test hypotheses where conservatism is one of the test variables, has been sustained across these alternative specifications.

$$\Delta E(t+1) = \beta 0 + \beta 1 \Delta E + \beta 2 \text{NEG} + \beta 3 \Delta \text{E} * \text{NEG} + \varepsilon, \tag{3.2}$$

Here, NEG identifies negative values for ΔE. Similar to the interpretation of the first model, the coefficients in this regression can be understood as follows: β1 represents the persistence of earnings increases, the sum of coefficients β1 and β3 represents the persistence of earnings declines, and β3 indicates the strength of the asymmetry in the persistence of increases versus declines. Basu's (1997) results are consistent with negative earnings changes exhibiting a greater tendency to revert in the next period than positive earnings changes.[4]

The Basu (1997) model has profoundly influenced subsequent accounting research, not only due to its theoretical insights but also for providing empirical researchers with a measure of conditional conservatism (β3) that can vary across firms. This variability enables testing whether certain samples exhibit higher conservatism than others. Ryan (2006, p. 513) emphasized the model's significance, stating that "Basu (1997) is easily one of the most influential papers in accounting research in the past decade." Ryan (2006, p. 514) further noted that "the largest concentration of [papers citing Basu, 1997] hypothesize and usually find that the extent of conditional conservatism, as measured by asymmetric timeliness, varies across firms' characteristics, choices, and economic contexts in a fashion consistent with the magnitude of the contracting and incentive issues involved and how the firm has addressed them." This suggests that the model is primarily employed to test hypotheses where conservatism is the dependent variable, exploring its determinants. Early research may have favored explaining the drivers of conservatism rather than its consequences. However, it is worth noting that the model, measuring conservatism by the coefficient β3 in Eq. (3.1), is particularly suited to test how a given determinant (VAR) affects conservatism through the following augmented regression equation:

$$\begin{aligned}\text{EARN} = {} & \beta 0 + \beta 1 \text{VAR} + \beta 2 \text{RET} + \beta 3 \text{VAR} * \text{RET} + \beta 4 \text{NEG} \\ & + \beta 5 \text{VAR} * \text{NEG} + \beta 6 \text{RET} * \text{NEG} + \beta 7 \text{VAR} * \text{RET} * \text{NEG} + \varepsilon\end{aligned} \tag{3.3}$$

Indeed, it is common practice to test the association between conservatism and a given test variable (VAR) by augmenting the Basu (1997) model in the way described above. In this setup, the significance of the coefficient β7 is examined to assess the hypothesis that VAR is associated with conservatism. β7 represents how the asymmetric timeliness coefficient varies as VAR increases.

In contrast, employing the model to test hypotheses where conservatism is the independent variable may present challenges. This difficulty arises because the

[4] An implication of this finding is that, if investors understand the effects that conservatism has on the asymmetric persistence of profits and losses, then the 3-day reaction to the announcement of an earnings increase should be stronger than the reaction to an earnings decline, because the latter is more likely to be reverting in the future. Consistent with this intuition, Basu (1997) shows than the market reaction to earnings changes is stronger when earnings are increasing, a finding also consistent with subsequent literature (e.g., Bartov et al., 2002; Lopez & Rees, 2002).

coefficient β3 is not a firm-year-specific variable but can only be measured on a sample of observations. Researchers have proposed various solutions to overcome this challenge. For instance, Kim and Pevzner (2010) estimated a firm-specific β3 by running Eq. (3.1) on a rolling window of 12 firm-years. Alternatively, the model can be used to test whether conservatism is stronger among firms that will later exhibit higher values of a given dependent variable, DVAR, by replacing VAR with DVAR in Eq. (3.3) (e.g., D'Augusta et al., 2016; Francis & Martin, 2010; Kim & Zhang, 2016). More recently, Barth et al. (2020) proposed using a latent class model to group observations within each year into homogeneous classes for Eq. (3.1).

3.2 An Alternative Approach: Ball and Shivakumar (2005)

Ball and Shivakumar (2005) analyzed the quality of financial reporting of private UK companies, drawing on the conceptual framework established by Basu (1997) to measure reporting quality with asymmetric loss recognition timeliness (i.e., conditional conservatism). However, their study encountered a challenge: it is infeasible to utilize coefficient β3 in Basu's regression Eq. (3.1) to measure conservatism among private companies due to the unavailability of a critical variable, namely stock market returns. Ball and Shivakumar (2005) employed two alternative approaches to address this issue.

Firstly, as the earnings time series of private companies are available from financial statements' data, they utilized the asymmetric earnings persistence measure (i.e., coefficient β3 in Eq. 3.2) to gauge conservatism. However, Ball and Shivakumar (2005, p. 93) acknowledged two limitations of this approach. They noted that it fails to differentiate between earnings' transitory gain or loss components and random errors in accruals or certain types of earnings management that lead to negative serial dependence on earnings changes. Additionally, while the model identifies the recognition of transitory earnings components, it does not address whether this recognition is timely or untimely.

Secondly, in response to the limitations above, Ball and Shivakumar (2005) developed a new model based on the likelihood that loss recognition timeliness occurs through accounting accruals. Prior research (e.g., Dechow, 1994; Dechow et al., 1998) had underscored the role of accruals in attenuating noise in cash flows from operations. For instance, large inventory purchases temporarily decrease cash holdings, which revert as inventory is sold in future periods. Recognizing inventory as an asset upon purchase and as an expense upon sale mitigates the effects of such purchases on reported performance, generating a negative association between current cash flows and accruals.

Ball and Shivakumar (2005) proposed a secondary role for accruals: the asymmetric recognition of good and bad news into earnings. Economic bad news can lead to a negative revision in both current and future cash flows. For instance, if a company's products become obsolete due to a competitor's innovation, the company may have to sell current inventory at a discount and anticipate selling future products at similar discounts. Both effects are reflected in current earnings: the shock to current cash flows through the cash component (e.g., lower cash receipts from customers) and the shock to future cash flows through the accrual components (e.g., recording impairment losses for unsold inventory or the assets used to produce it). This results in a positive association between current cash flows and accruals.

Conversely, economic good news can lead to a positive revision in current and future cash flows (e.g., the company's ability to sell its products at higher margins). However, due to the lower timeliness of recognizing good news in earnings, only the current effect is incorporated into earnings through higher current cash receipts. The revision to future cash flows is not recognized through accruals but is delayed until future cash flows are realized, thus being incorporated into future earnings through higher future cash receipts. Therefore, the second role of accruals generates a positive association between cash flows and accruals when news is bad but not when news is good. In other words, asymmetric recognition timeliness results in an asymmetric association between current cash flows and accruals: the association is less negative for negative cash flows, where the two roles of accruals—noise mitigation and bad news recognition—offset each other than for positive accruals, where the predominant role of accruals is to mitigate cash flow variations.

Ball and Shivakumar (2005) adopted a model akin to Basu's (1997) equation to measure conservatism using the new approach. Specifically, they regressed current accruals (ACCR) on current cash flows (CF), allowing the coefficient of CF to vary depending on whether CF is negative (i.e., NEG = 1), as shown in the following model:

$$\mathrm{ACCR} = \beta 0 + \beta 1\mathrm{CF} + \beta 2\mathrm{NEG} + \beta 3\mathrm{CF} * \mathrm{NEG} + \varepsilon \tag{3.4}$$

In this equation, the coefficient β1 is expected to be negative because it represents the association between cash flows and accruals when cash flow is positive (i.e., accruals are negative to mitigate the positive increase in cash). The sum of coefficients β1 and β3 is expected to be less negative than β1 alone, indicating that when cash flow is negative, some accruals are positive to mitigate the negative cash flow, while others are negative to account for future losses. Consequently, β3 is expected to be positive and serves as the measure of asymmetric timeliness that captures conservatism in a sample of firms.

Using the Ball and Shivakumar (2005) model to test the association of conservatism with a certain variable VAR follows a procedure similar to that described above for the Basu (1997) model. Researchers can estimate the coefficients of the following equation:

$$\begin{aligned}\mathrm{ACCR} = {} & \beta 0 + \beta 1\mathrm{VAR} + \beta 2\mathrm{CF} + \beta 3\mathrm{VAR} * \mathrm{CF} + \beta 4\mathrm{NEG} \\ & + \beta 5\mathrm{VAR} * \mathrm{NEG} + \beta 6\mathrm{CF} * \mathrm{NEG} + \beta 7\mathrm{VAR} * \mathrm{CF} * \mathrm{NEG} + \varepsilon\end{aligned} \tag{3.5}$$

In this equation, the estimate of coefficient β7 provides a test of the association between conservatism and the variable of interest VAR.

Following Ball and Shivakumar's (2005) contribution, numerous papers have embraced this approach to investigate conditional conservatism. This model is well-suited for studying conservatism in private firms as it does not rely on market-based variables such as stock returns. For example, Cameran et al. (2014) utilized it to explore differences in conservatism between adopters of International Financial Reporting Standards (IFRS) and non-adopters. Cano-Rodríguez (2010) employed it to analyze the effect of a large auditor on the conditional conservatism of Spanish private firms. However, other papers, like Chi et al. (2013), followed Ball and Shivakumar in utilizing Basu's (1997) asymmetric persistence model (i.e., augmenting Eq. 3.2) to study conservatism among private firms.

The mentioned papers utilized Ball and Shivakumar's (2005) model to investigate the determinants of conservatism among private firms, treating conservatism as a dependent construct that can vary based on factors such as IFRS adoption or auditor size. Due to reasons similar to those discussed in the previous section, the model lends itself well to this approach since it allows the interaction of an independent variable VAR with the term CF*NEG, enabling the coefficient β3 to serve as the dependent variable. However, using the model to test hypotheses where conservatism is the independent construct (i.e., studying the consequences of conservatism on other variables) can be challenging.

In other words, while offering a valuable alternative to Basu's (1997) models for testing conservatism among private firms, the Ball and Shivakumar (2005) approach does not aim to provide a firm-year-specific measure that can be easily employed as a standalone independent variable. The models discussed in the following paragraphs address this issue by proposing approaches to obtain such a firm-year-specific proxy.

3.3 Firm-Year-Specific Measures of Conditional Conservatism

3.3.1 Khan and Watts (2009)

In a highly influential paper, Khan and Watts (2009) introduced a method to estimate conservatism using a firm-year measure. They empirically assessed the properties of this metric and explored its potential applications, particularly in examining the nature and effects of conservatism. Their study validated the efficacy of the measure in capturing variations in conservatism and its ability to predict asymmetric earnings timeliness up to 3 years in advance. Since then, this metric has become widely adopted in empirical accounting research for its capability to capture the degree of conservatism of the financial reports of a given firm in a given year.

The model is based on the Basu (1997) cross-sectional regression equation, specified as per Eq. (3.1). To estimate the asymmetric timeliness at a firm-year level, Khan and Watts (2009) specified a model where good news timeliness (i.e., coefficient β1 in Eq. (3.1), labeled as "GSCORE") and asymmetric timeliness (i.e., coefficient β3 in Eq. 3.1, labeled as "CSCORE") are linear functions of three observable firm-specific characteristics, namely firm size, market-to-book ratio, and financial leverage. After running annual cross-sectional regressions of the model, the value of CSCORE for each firm-year can be obtained as the predicted value of the coefficient β3 based on the three variables' observable values.

Despite its popularity, CSCORE is not without limitations. Khan and Watts (2009) cautioned that empirical studies investigating conservatism and utilizing CSCORE as a dependent or independent variable in regression analysis may require controlling for additional factors such as the market-to-book ratio, leverage, or size. Neglecting to account for these variables, which are components of the CSCORE calculation, could lead to the identification of an association between conservatism (as measured by CSCORE) and the variable under scrutiny, even when no such association exists.

More recently, Byzalov and Basu (2023) argued that using x-Score analysis, such as the Khan and Watts' (2009) model, may result in biased coefficients and pose challenges in interpretation because it fails to account for additional sources of variation and the estimates often rely on undisclosed technical assumptions. They cautioned against using this approach to proxy for dependent variables in regression models and demonstrate that significant findings in published literature may change once the bias is corrected.

Given these issues, various empirical studies have adopted a research design based on multiple firm-year-specific proxies to test the robustness of their findings. The following paragraphs discuss some of the most commonly adopted proxies.

3.3.2 Callen et al. (2010)

When measuring conservatism at the firm-specific level to model it as an explanatory variable, several studies have adopted the conservatism ratio (CR) developed by Callen et al. (2010). This measure is based on the nonlinear relationship between unexpected equity returns and earnings news, defined as the expected current and future earnings change. Drawing from this framework, they devised a ratio representing the proportion of the total shock to expected current and future earnings recognized in the current year's earnings.

Callen et al. (2010) validated their proxy by ranking firms based on it and showing that firms with higher values of the ratio exhibit characteristics such as increased leverage, greater return volatility, higher incidence of losses, more negative accruals, and heightened volatility of earnings and accruals, aligning with theoretical expectations based on existing literature.

Several studies have utilized Callen et al.'s (2010) measure to assess a firm's annual earnings conservatism. For example, Biddle et al. (2022) incorporated it, among other measures, to investigate whether conditional conservatism helps mitigate bankruptcy risk. Similarly, D'Augusta and Redigolo (2019) employed it to examine the association between the downward effect of conservatism in current earnings and the firm's propensity to release early guidance about future earnings trends. Additionally, García Lara et al. (2020) conducted tests on the relationship between conservatism and firms' ability to manipulate earnings, using various proxies, including Callen et al.'s (2010) measure.

However, a potential issue when adopting this proxy, as noted by Callen et al. (2010), is that negative values of CR pose interpretation challenges. Specifically, instances where earnings news is negative despite a positive current period earnings shock may indicate excessively optimistic financial reporting. Conversely, situations where earnings news is positive but the shock is negative might suggest overly cautious financial reporting practices. Furthermore, according to Callen et al.'s (2010) model, a firm demonstrates greater conservatism than another if it recognizes more of a negative shock and less of a positive one. Therefore, the interpretation of CR's coefficient depends on the shock sign. Consequently, some empirical studies using Callen et al.'s (2010) measure have multiplied the ratio by negative one for positive news so that higher values represent greater conservatism (Biddle et al., 2022).

3.3.3 *Givoly and Hayn (2000), and Other Time-Series Measures*

Givoly and Hayn (2000) analyzed whether changes in the patterns of earnings, cash flows, and accruals over time are indicative of increased reporting conservatism. One aspect they investigated was the change in the skewness of earnings and cash flow distributions. They argued that "if conservatism leads to an immediate and complete recognition of negative events and a delayed and gradual recognition of positive events, it is likely to result in a negatively skewed earnings distribution" (Givoly & Hayn, 2000, p. 293). In contrast, cash flow distribution properties are unlikely to be affected by conservatism.

Their analysis spanning the last four decades of the twentieth century revealed an increasingly negative skewness of earnings compared to cash flow distribution. Additionally, they observed a near-monotonic accumulation of negative accruals starting from 1982, indicating that net income before depreciation was consistently lower than cash flows from operations. The growing negative skewness of earnings and the accumulation of negative non-operating accruals are consistent with increased conservatism over time.

Subsequent empirical studies have extended Givoly and Hayn's (2000) insights to measure conservatism. Many studies have measured the average level of conservatism across observations using either the difference between the skewness of earnings and cash flows or the average accumulation of negative accruals. At the firm-year level, this is often achieved by calculating the difference in skewness values of quarterly earnings and cash flows, or the average absolute value of non-operating accruals, over a rolling window of several years before or centered on the year of interest. Various empirical papers have adopted either (or both) of Givoly and Hayn's (2000) accrual-based proxies to study conservatism's effects on the stock market (e.g., D'Augusta, 2022; Garcìa Lara et al., 2014; García Lara et al., 2020; Kim et al., 2013).

However, some limitations of Givoly and Hayn's (2000) measures have been identified. Questions have been raised regarding whether the accumulation of negative accruals effectively isolates conditional conservatism or reflects, at least in part, unconditional conservatism as well (Garcìa Lara et al., 2007). This aspect may well be consistent with the research question under test. For instance, Chen, Chen, and Cheng (2014) investigated the impact of founding family ownership on conservatism. They measured conservatism with non-operating accruals averaged over the 3 years centered on the year of interest, and they argued that this measure "captures both conditional and unconditional conservatism, consistent with [their] conceptual focus on total conservatism" (Chen, Chen, & Cheng, 2014, p. 411).

Additionally, these measures require a relatively long time window, potentially limiting data availability and biasing the sample toward older firms. Similar challenges arise with measures that apply the Basu (1997) or Ball and Shivakumar (2005) models over a firm-specific rolling window before the year when the conservatism proxy is measured, risking measurement error due to small sample size and noise. Despite these limitations, these approaches have been utilized in the literature, often in combination with other measures (Francis et al., 2013; Kim & Pevzner, 2010; Zhang, 2008).

3.3.4 *Composite Measures*

Empirical researchers have typically employed models incorporating multiple firm-year conservatism proxies discussed above. However, a challenge to this approach arises from the possibility that different conservatism measures may capture distinct aspects of conservatism with error (Chen, Folsom, et al., 2014; Hui et al., 2009). Research indeed indicates a rather low correlation among these proxies. For example, Kim and Pevzner (2010, Table 1) reported that the correlation between a time-series conservatism measure based on the Basu (1997) model and three other conservatism proxies ranged between insignificance and 0.037. Similarly, Kim et al. (2013, Table 4) reported that Khan and Watt's (2009) CSCORE's correlation with the two accrual-based measures developed by Givoly and Hayn (2000) was either insignificant or lower than 5%, and Sohn (2012) showed the same correlations to be either insignificant or negative. Kim and Pevzner (2010, p. 320) argued that these low correlations may indicate "the potential noisy nature of conservatism variables."

Various studies have adopted a composite measure based on the average decile (or other quantile) rank of two or more firm-year-specific variables to overcome potential limitations due to the low correlation among the conservatism proxies. These combined measures are "intended to better capture the overall level of a firm's reporting conservatism" (Mashruwala & Mashruwala, 2018, p. 2162) compared to individual proxies. For instance, Aier et al. (2014) employed this approach when examining debtholders' demand for conservatism. Similarly, this methodology was utilized by D'Augusta and DeAngelis (2020) to test conservatism's role in disciplining qualitative disclosures, by Kim et al. (2013) to demonstrate conservatism's effect on stock market returns around seasoned equity offerings, and by Ettredge et al. (2016) to examine the association of conservatism with subsequent initiation of lawsuits. Another approach to achieve a similar end is to employ factor analysis to obtain an aggregate measure of different conservatism scores, as seen in Chen, Folsom, et al. (2014) or Hui et al. (2009).

3.4 The Debate About the Basu's (1997) Model

Following the publication of Basu (1997), estimating conservatism using the asymmetric timeliness coefficient became very popular among empirical researchers. However, criticism of the model and its ability to capture conservatism soon emerged. One of the earliest critiques pointing out conceptual and empirical flaws with the model was presented by Dietrich et al. (2007). They argued that unless very restrictive conditions are met, the test statistics of the asymmetric timeliness estimation procedure will be biased, resulting in spurious evidence of conservatism. A significant source of the bias is that in the Basu (1997) model regression equation, stock returns and earnings are, respectively, the independent and dependent variables, despite earnings being a driver of returns along with other non-accounting sources. They contended that the bias is irresolvable because it stems from the Basu (1997) model's test specification, and the severity of this bias precludes using asymmetric timeliness tests to measure conservatism accurately.

Around the same time as Dietrich et al. (2007), another paper by Givoly et al. (2007) raised significant concerns about whether the Basu (1997) model is well-suited to capture conservatism. Unlike Dietrich et al. (2007), Givoly et al. (2007) assumed the Basu (1997) model was valid, but they questioned its asymmetric timeliness measure's power and reliability to capture conservatism. They argued that three factors not related to reporting conservatism are likely to affect the magnitude of the measure. The first is the aggregation effect, resulting from using aggregated data (i.e., annual earnings and annual stock returns) to estimate the asymmetric timeliness measure, impairing the tests' power and ability to detect conservatism when it is present. The second is the nature of the economic events effect, which stems from some economic events not being recognized in earnings regardless of conservatism. This leads to overstating (understating) the conservatism measurement when there is a preponderance of favorable (unfavorable) events of this type. Finally, the disclosure policy effect is because firms can be conservative in their disclosure rather than recognition decisions, but disclosure is one of the main channels through which earnings news is priced under the assumption of semi-strong market efficiency. Therefore, holding reporting conservatism constant, the faster disclosure of good (bad) news relative to its recognition will lead to the asymmetric timeliness measure overstating (understating) conservatism.

A few years later, a third article raised additional concerns regarding the estimates of conservatism based on the Basu (1997) asymmetric timeliness model, suggesting they suffer from bias. Patatoukas and Thomas (2011) cautioned that two empirical patterns associated with scale bias estimates of conservatism derived from asymmetric timeliness. The first pattern stems from a positive correlation between scale and price-deflated earnings, termed the loss effect due to its association with firms reporting losses. The second pattern, labeled the return variance effect, arises from a negative correlation between scale and stock return variance. Patatoukas and Thomas (2011) highlighted that shifts in these empirical patterns significantly influence changes in the conservatism measure across different samples. To detect evidence of bias, they employed a placebo test approach, replicating the Basu (1997) model using prior year earnings instead of current ones. Patatoukas and Thomas (2011, p. 1766) argued that "as last year's earnings cannot reflect news that will be revealed subsequently this year, it cannot differentially reflect the good and bad components of this year's news, and the [asymmetric timeliness] estimate should therefore be zero." However, they found evidence of asymmetric timeliness of lagged earnings, with over 60% of that for current earnings, consistent with bias.

Banker et al. (2016) subsequently raised a fourth set of concerns. They noted that the impact of sales decreases on earnings is greater than that of sales increases due to cost stickiness. This, they argued, threatens the reliability of the Basu (1997) model in capturing conservatism, as changes in sales can be an omitted variable confounding asymmetrical timeliness coefficient estimates. They demonstrated that controlling for a piecewise linear effect of sales changes in the model significantly reduces estimates of conservatism levels and cross-sectional variation with other variables. While Banker et al. (2016, p. 216) did "not refute the general approach of using (appropriately corrected) asymmetric timeliness as a measure of conditional conservatism" because "after controlling for sticky costs, asymmetric timeliness estimates are in agreement with conservatism theory," their findings suggest that conservatism estimates based on the original Basu (1997) model can be distorted by cost stickiness if left uncontrolled for.

In response to these concerns, various papers have revisited the econometrics and empirical properties of the Basu (1997) model, offering alternative solutions. For instance, Ball et al. (2013) challenged Patatoukas and Thomas's (2011) suggestion to avoid conditional conservatism estimates based on the Basu (1997) model. They argue that the bias highlighted by Patatoukas and Thomas (2011) stems from a correlated omitted variables problem, arising from the fact that the "correlation between the expected components of earnings and returns biases estimates of how earnings incorporate the information contained in returns" (Ball et al., 2013, p. 755). Ball et al. proposed modifying the model to incorporate unexpected earnings (returns) as the dependent (independent) variable or simply including firm fixed effects to address this issue.

Collins et al. (2014) contended that accrual and operating cash flow contribute to earnings' asymmetric timeliness, but only accruals reflect a firm's conservative accounting. They argued that operating cash flows do not reflect differential verification thresholds for recognizing uncertain profits or losses, making cash-flow asymmetry a source of noise or bias in conservatism tests based on the Basu (1997) model. Accordingly, Collins et al. (2014) demonstrated that using accruals instead of earnings as the dependent variable of the Basu (1997) model mitigates many of the biases identified by prior literature and yields conservatism estimates consistent with theory.

Expanding on the work of Ball et al. (2013), Badia et al. (2021) proposed four modifications to the Basu (1997) model to address the sources of bias identified by prior literature. Specifically, they recommended (1) using unexpected earnings as the dependent variable and unexpected returns in the interactive explanatory variables, (2) including firm fixed effects in the regression equation, (3) adding interactive controls for return variance, and (4) embedding interactive controls for the market-to-book ratio of assets. They suggested that "these modifications directly address and largely eliminate the known biases in Basu's [conservatism] measure" (Badia et al., 2021, p. 1225).

3.5 Measurement of Other Forms of Conservatism

3.5.1 Unconditional Conservatism

Penman and Zhang (2002, 242) introduced an index of unconditional conservatism, labeled C-Score,[5] "based on the accounting treatment of three investments for which the accounting is relatively immune from managerial discretion after the expenditure has occurred: inventories, R&D, and advertising." Specifically, their measure is calculated as the level of estimated reserves created by conservatism relative to net operating assets. While this measure captures the effect of conservative accounting on the balance sheet, the effect on the income statement can be proxied by the average of (1) the year-over-year change in C-Score and (2) the difference between a firm's C-Score and the industry median. Penman and Zhang's (2002) C-Score has been extensively adopted in the literature (e.g., Biddle et al., 2022; Hui et al., 2009; Jaggi et al., 2021).

[5] Despite being labeled in the same way, the reader must be careful not to confuse this proxy with the one developed by Khan and Watts (2009), which is a proxy for the expected value of *conditional* conservatism in a given firm-year.

Another measure of unconditional conservatism is based on the concept that this form of conservatism results in a persistent downward bias in book value (Beaver & Ryan, 2000). For example, Qiang (2007) proxied unconditional conservatism with an inverse estimate of the intercept from a regression of the book-to-market ratio on lagged returns, allowing for a different slope for positive and negative returns, similar to Basu (1997).

3.5.2 *Balance Sheet Conservatism and Non-discretionary Conservatism*

Sunder et al. (2018, p.497) defined balance sheet conservatism as "the difference between book value and market value of assets reported on the balance sheet due to the cumulative effects of past conservative accounting." They measured it by conducting a regression of the book-to-market ratio on various explanatory variables that capture growth and economic rents, distress, market sentiment, unrealized mark-to-market gains, and inflation. They argued that if these variables control for other known drivers of the book-to-market ratio, then the residual from the regression will serve as a proxy for balance sheet conservatism. To validate their measure, they showed that it increases in various proxies for unconditional conservatism (e.g., accelerated depreciation, R&D, and advertising reserves). Additionally, they showed that past conditional conservatism increases balance sheet conservatism, which in turn constrains future conditional conservatism, aligning with Roychowdhury and Watts' (2007) findings of an asymmetric association between conditional conservatism and end-of-period and beginning-of-period market-to-book ratios.

Lawrence et al. (2013) asserted that compliance with Generally Accepted Accounting Principles (GAAP) plays a significant role in explaining cross-sectional variation in conservatism, defining conservatism required by accounting rules as non-discretionary. They showed a positive and nonlinear association between the beginning-of-period book-to-market ratio and asset write-downs, particularly pronounced for firms with weaker performance and those with a higher proportion of intangible assets. Their findings underscored the importance of proxying for non-discretionary conservatism using the beginning book-to-market ratio to control for its impact in conditional conservatism tests.

References

Aier, J. K., Chen, L., & Pevzner, M. (2014). Debtholders' demand for conservatism: Evidence from changes in directors' fiduciary duties. *Journal of Accounting Research, 52*(5), 993–1027.

Badia, M., Duro, M., Penalva, F., & Ryan, S. G. (2021). Debiasing the measurement of conditional conservatism. *Journal of Accounting Research, 59*(4), 1221–1259.

Ball, R., Kothari, S. P., & Nikolaev, V. (2013). On estimating conditional conservatism. *The Accounting Review, 88*(3), 755–787.

Ball, R., Kothari, S. P., & Robin, A. (2000). The effect of international institutional factors on properties of accounting earnings. *Journal of Accounting and Economics, 29*, 1–51.

Ball, R., Robin, A., & Sadka, G. (2008). Is financial reporting shaped by equity markets or by debt markets? An international study of timeliness and conservatism. *Review of Accounting Studies, 13*(2–3), 168–205.

Ball, R., & Shivakumar, L. (2005). Earnings quality in UK private firms: Comparative loss recognition timeliness. *Journal of Accounting and Economics, 39*(1), 83–128.

Banker, R., Basu, S., Byzalov, D., & Chen, J. Y. S. (2016). The confounding effect of cost stickiness on conservatism estimates. *Journal of Accounting and Economics, 61*(1), 203–220.

Barth, M. E., Landsman, W. R., Raval, V., & Wang, S. (2020). Asymmetric timeliness and the resolution of investor disagreement and uncertainty at earnings announcements. *The Accounting Review, 95*(4), 23–50.

Bartov, E., Givoly, D., & Hayn, C. (2002). The rewards to meeting or beating earnings expectations. *Journal of Accounting and Economics, 33*, 173–204.

Basu, S. (1995). *Conservatism and the asymmetric timeliness of earnings*. Ph.D. dissertation, University of Rochester.

Basu, S. (1997). The conservatism principle and the asymmetric timeliness of earnings. *Journal of Accounting and Economics, 24*(1), 3–37.

Beaver, W. H., & Ryan, S. G. (2000). Biases and lags in book value and their effects on the ability of the book-to-market ratio to predict book return on equity. *Journal of Accounting Research, 38*(1), 127–148.

Beaver, W. H., & Ryan, S. G. (2005). Conditional and unconditional conservatism: Concepts and modeling. *Review of Accounting Studies, 10*(2–3), 269–309.

Biddle, G. C., Ma, M. L. Z., & Song, F. M. (2022). Accounting conservatism and bankruptcy risk. *Journal of Accounting, Auditing & Finance, 37*(2), 295–323.

Byzalov, D., & Basu, S. (2023). The misuse of regression-based x-scores as dependent variables. *Journal of Accounting and Economics, 77*, 101643.

Callen, J. L., Segal, D., & Hope, O.-K. (2010). The pricing of conservative accounting and the measurement of conservatism at the firm-year level. *Review of Accounting Studies, 15*(1), 145–178.

Cameran, M., Campa, D., & Pettinicchio, A. (2014). IFRS adoption among private companies. *Journal of Accounting, Auditing & Finance, 29*(3), 278–305.

Cano-Rodríguez, M. (2010). Big auditors, private firms and accounting conservatism: Spanish evidence. *European Accounting Review, 19*(1), 131–159.

Chen, S., Chen, X., & Cheng, Q. (2014). Conservatism and equity ownership of the founding family. *European Accounting, 23*(3), 403–430.

Chen, L. H., Folsom, D., Paek, W., & Sami, H. (2014). Accounting conservatism, earnings persistence and pricing multiples on earnings. *Accounting Horizons, 28*(2), 233–260.

Chi, W., Dhaliwal, D., Li, O. Z., & Lin, T. H. (2013). Voluntary reporting incentives and reporting quality: Evidence from a reporting regime change for private firms in Taiwan. *Contemporary Accounting Research, 30*(4), 1462–1489.

Collins, D. W., Hribar, P., & Tian, X. (2014). Cash flow asymmetry: Causes and implications for conditional conservatism research. *Journal of Accounting and Economics, 58*(2–3), 173–200.

D'Augusta, C. (2022). Does accounting conservatism make good news forecasts more credible and bad news forecasts less alarming? *Journal of Accounting, Auditing & Finance, 37*(1), 77–113.

D'Augusta, C., Bar-Yosef, S., & Prencipe, A. (2016). The effects of conservative reporting on investor disagreement. *European Accounting Review, 25*(3), 451–485.

D'Augusta, C., & DeAngelis, M. D. (2020). Does accounting conservatism discipline qualitative disclosure? Evidence from tone management in the MD&A. *Contemporary Accounting Research, 37*(4), 2287–2318.

D'Augusta, C., & Redigolo, G. (2019). Do firms use early guidance to disclose the effect of conservatism on future earnings? *Review of Accounting and Finance, 18*(3), 432–455.

Dechow, P. M. (1994). Accounting earnings and cash flows as measures of firm performance: The role of accounting accruals. *Journal of Accounting and Economics, 18*(1), 3–42.
Dechow, P. M., Kothari, S. P., & Watts, R. L. (1998). The relation between earnings and cash flows. pdf. *Journal of Accounting and Economics, 25*, 133–168.
Dietrich, J. R., Muller, K. A., & Riedl, E. J. (2007). Asymmetric timeliness tests of accounting conservatism. *Review of Accounting Studies, 12*(1), 95–124.
Ettredge, M. L., Huang, Y., & Zhang, W. (2016). Conservative reporting and securities class action lawsuits. *Accounting Horizons, 30*(1), 93–118.
Francis, B., Hasan, I., & Wu, Q. (2013). The benefits of conservative accounting to shareholders: Evidence from the financial crisis. *Accounting Horizons, 27*(2), 319–349.
Francis, J. R., & Martin, X. (2010). Acquisition profitability and timely loss recognition. *Journal of Accounting and Economics, 49*(1–2), 161–178.
Garcìa Lara, J. M., Garcìa Osma, B., & Penalva, F. (2007). Accounting conservatism and corporate governance. *Review of Accounting Studies, 14*(1), 161–201.
Garcìa Lara, J. M., Garcìa Osma, B., & Penalva, F. (2014). Information consequences of accounting conservatism. *European Accounting Review, 23*(2), 173–198.
García Lara, J. M., García Osma, B., & Penalva, F. (2020). Conditional conservatism and the limits to earnings management. *Journal of Accounting and Public Policy, 39*(4), 106738.
Givoly, D., & Hayn, C. (2000). The changing time-series properties of earnings, cash flows and accruals: Has financial reporting become more conservative? *Journal of Accounting and Economics, 29*(3), 287–320.
Givoly, D., Hayn, C., & Natarajan, A. (2007). Measuring reporting conservatism. *The Accounting Review, 82*(1), 65–106.
Hui, K. W., Matsunaga, S. R., & Morse, D. (2009). The impact of conservatism on management earnings forecasts. *Journal of Accounting and Economics, 47*(3), 192–207.
Jaggi, B., Ronen, J., & Xin, H. (2021). Management earnings forecast and accounting conservatism. *Journal of Accounting, Auditing & Finance, 36*(3), 451–474.
Khan, M., & Watts, R. L. (2009). Estimation and empirical properties of a firm-year measure of accounting conservatism. *Journal of Accounting and Economics, 48*(2–3), 132–150.
Kim, Y., Li, S., Pan, C., & Zuo, L. (2013). The role of accounting conservatism in the equity market: Evidence from seasoned equity offerings. *The Accounting Review, 88*(4), 1327–1356.
Kim, B. H., & Pevzner, M. (2010). Conditional accounting conservatism and future negative surprises: An empirical investigation. *Journal of Accounting and Public Policy, 29*(4), 311–329.
Kim, J.-B., & Zhang, L. (2016). Accounting conservatism and stock price crash risk: Firm-level evidence. *Contemporary Accounting Research, 33*(1), 412–441.
Lawrence, A., Sloan, R., & Sun, Y. (2013). Non-discretionary conservatism: Evidence and implications. *Journal of Accounting & Economics, 56*, 112–133.
Lee, H. S. G., Li, X., & Sami, H. (2015). Conditional conservatism and audit fees. *Accounting Horizons, 29*(1), 83–113.
Liu, Z., & Elayan, F. A. (2015). Litigation risk, information asymmetry and conditional conservatism. *Review of Quantitative Finance and Accounting, 44*(4), 581–608.
Lopez, T. J., & Rees, L. (2002). The effect of beating and missing analysts' forecasts on the information content of unexpected earnings. *Journal of Accounting, Auditing & Finance, 17*(2), 155–184.
Mashruwala, C., & Mashruwala, S. (2018). Does accounting conservatism reduce overpricing caused by short-sales constraints? *Contemporary Accounting Research, 35*(4), 2160–2190.
Pae, J., Thornton, D. B., & Welker, M. (2005). The link between earnings conservatism and the price to book ratio. *Contemporary Accounting Research, 22*(3), 693–717.
Patatoukas, P. N., & Thomas, J. K. (2011). More evidence of bias in the differential timeliness measure of conditional conservatism. *The Accounting Review, 86*(5), 1765–1793.
Penman, S. H., & Zhang, X.-J. (2002). Accounting conservatism, the quality of earnings, and stock returns. *The Accounting Review, 77*(2), 237–264.

Qiang, X. (2007). The effects of contracting, litigation, regulation, and tax costs on conditional and unconditional conservatism: Cross-sectional evidence at the firm level. *The Accounting Review, 82*(3), 759–796.

Roychowdhury, S., & Watts, R. L. (2007). Asymmetric timeliness of earnings, market-to-book and conservatism in financial reporting. *Journal of Accounting and Economics, 44*(1–2), 2–31.

Ryan, S. G. (2006). Identifying conditional conservatism. *European Accounting Review, 15*(4), 511–525.

Sohn, B. C. (2012). Analyst forecast, accounting conservatism and the related valuation implications. *Accounting & Finance, 52*(Suppl), 311–341.

Sunder, J., Sunder, S. V., & Zhang, J. (2018). Balance sheet conservatism and debt contracting. *Contemporary Accounting Research, 35*(1), 494–524.

Watts, R. L. (2003). Conservatism in accounting part I: Explanations and implications. *Accounting Horizons, 17*(3), 207–221.

Zhang, J. (2008). The contracting benefits of accounting conservatism to lenders and borrowers. *Journal of Accounting and Economics, 45*(1), 27–54.

Chapter 4
Conservatism and the Stock Market: Major Empirical Findings from Three Decades of Research

4.1 Conservatism, Agency Conflicts, and Corporate Governance

4.1.1 Researchers' New Interest in the Contracting Role of Conservatism

Toward the end of the twentieth century, there was a notable resurgence of interest among accounting scholars regarding the concept of conservatism, which would soon lead to a collective effort to deepen our understanding of its implications and applications in modern financial contexts. Spearheading this new wave of scholarly research, Basu (1997) revisited the conservatism concept, defining it as an asymmetry in the verification requirements of good and bad news in earnings. Shortly after, Watts (2003) theorized that contracting efficiency is one of the primary reasons for such an asymmetry. Watts (2003) argued that conservatism is instrumental in addressing moral hazard problems because different firm parties (e.g., managers, shareholders, and creditors) have asymmetric information and payoff functions, as well as limited horizons and liability. For instance, although creditors do not receive extra benefits when the firm's net assets surpass the debt's face value upon maturity, they are exposed to risks if the assets' value falls short of covering the agreed-upon payments. Consequently, debt holders are primarily concerned with preventing excessive asset distributions to shareholders that could jeopardize the firm's ability to honor debt payments. Conservatism helps mitigate the risk of excessive dividend payments, facilitating contracting between the firm and creditors.

Similarly, conservatism can help alleviate agency costs when shareholders and managers contract to determine managerial compensation. Without conservatism's constraint on reported earnings, managers may receive excessive compensation, resulting in reduced shareholder value. Furthermore, shareholders may be unable to recover these overpayments due to the manager's limited liability.

C. D'Augusta, *Accounting Conservatism and the Stock Market*, SpringerBriefs in Accounting, https://doi.org/10.1007/978-3-031-67145-6_4

An essential contribution to understanding the contracting role of conservatism came from the theoretical conceptualization of the distinction between the conditional and the unconditional form of conservatism (e.g., Beaver & Ryan, 2005).[1] It is the former form, which embodies Basu's (1997) interpretation of conservatism as asymmetric recognition timeliness, that, according to Ball and Shivakumar (2005), serves a contracting purpose because it increases the usefulness of financial statements' numbers in several contracting contexts, such as loan agreements or corporate governance contracts between shareholders and managers (i.e., management compensation agreements).

4.1.2 *Conservatism's Association with Corporate Governance and External Audit Quality*

The theoretical discussions above, highlighting conservatism's role in addressing agency conflicts, have prompted empirical researchers to explore how conservatism is linked with different corporate governance mechanisms that serve similar agency functions. For instance, Beekes et al. (2004) investigated the relationship between conditional conservatism and a company's board composition. They discovered that firms with more outside board members tend to promptly recognize bad news, though they found no such effect regarding good news. Similarly, Ahmed and Duellman (2007) showed a positive correlation between conservatism and board characteristics indicative of board independence and monitoring incentives for outside directors. Additionally, Garcìa Lara et al. (2007) revealed that firms with stronger corporate governance, as measured by internal and external board characteristics, tend to exhibit higher levels of conservatism.

Other studies have focused on conservatism's connection with external audit services. For instance, Chung et al. (2003) found that Big Auditors can induce conditional conservatism in underperforming clients. This positive relationship between audit quality and conditional conservatism has been confirmed internationally. Francis and Wang (2008) showed that conservatism is influenced by both the investor protection environment and the choice of a Big Four versus a non-Big Four auditor. Similarly, Cano-Rodrígue z (2010) showed that large auditors enhance contracting efficiency by promoting conditional conservatism in Spanish firms, even with minimal incentives for independence. However, in high-risk scenarios, they tend to increase unconditional conservatism, potentially compromising financial report quality. Additionally, Cameran et al. (2016) examined changes in audit quality over the auditor engagement period in a context with mandatory audit firm rotation (Italy). They found evidence of increasing auditor-induced conservatism in the last 3-year period preceding mandatory rotation.

---

[1] See Chap. 2.

4.1.3 Conservatism's Governance Role in Resolving Firm-Debtholders Conflicts

Therefore, between the beginning and the mid-2000s, accounting research developed theoretical arguments for the corporate governance role of conservatism in resolving conflicts between contracting parties such as managers, shareholders, and creditors. This allowed hypothesizing that conservatism arises from the demand of (and therefore is likely to impact) *both* the debt and stock markets. Indeed, in the second part of that decade, empirical researchers dedicated significant effort to investigating the former link between conservatism and the debt market; conservatism's relationship with the stock market, however, did not initially enjoy the same focus.

Among the contributions exploring the benefits of conservatism for lenders in the early 2000s, Ahmed et al. (2002) examined whether conservatism helps resolve the conflict between shareholders and debtholders over dividend policy. The conflict arises because creditors face the risk that excessive dividend payouts to shareholders will damage the firm's financial position and ultimately impair its ability to meet financial obligations. Ahmed et al. (2002) found that conservatism plays an important role in mitigating the bondholder–shareholder conflicts over dividend policy and reducing firms' debt costs.

However, a later paper by Gigler et al. (2009) suggested that conservatism can decrease the efficiency of debt contracts. The inefficiency is linked to conservatism's effect on earnings' information content. Gigler et al. (2009) used the following metaphor to illustrate their point: "A very stringent scoring policy would make it almost impossible for low-ability students to score a high grade of A, but it inevitably results in some high-ability students also scoring a low grade of B. Thus, a high grade is very informative; students scoring an A are very likely to be high-ability/high-knowledge students. But a low grade of B contains a mixed signal since some high-ability students, in addition to most low-ability students, are awarded a B grade." This argument is interesting because it also applies to the debate on the information consequences of conservatism for stock market investors.

Among other studies analyzing lenders' demand for conservatism in the first decade of the century, Beatty et al. (2008) investigated whether the firm can satisfy creditors' demand for conservatism by agreeing to conservative contract modifications rather than by increasing reporting conservatism. They showed that such modifications are more likely when agency costs are higher and other conservatism demand sources are lower (e.g., shareholders' demand). Zhang (2008) argued that conservatism benefits creditors ex post by providing timely signals of default risk and helps firms ex ante by allowing them to enjoy more favorable credit terms. Consistent with this argument, Zhang (2008) found that more conservative borrowers are more likely to violate debt covenants in response to price shocks, and they are offered better interest rates by lenders.

Another paper investigating conservatism's association with the debt market by focusing on debt covenants is Nikolaev (2010), who examined whether more frequent use of covenants in firms' public debt contracts is associated with timelier recognition of losses in earnings. Nikolaev (2010) argued that if covenants aim to protect creditors by transferring control rights from shareholders when the company approaches financial hardship, such a goal can be achieved only when the reporting system promptly recognizes bad news. Consistent with this intuition, Nikolaev (2010) showed that loss recognition is timelier among firms that use covenants more extensively.

The studies above illustrate how, in the first decade of the twenty-first century, the accounting research community invested considerable efforts to comprehend the cause-and-effect relationships between conservatism and the debt market. Concurrently, accounting researchers began exploring certain aspects of the association between conservatism and the stock market, such as examining the international context or disparities between public and private firms. However, the inquiry into whether stock market dynamics influence conservatism and the effects of conservatism on stock market investors received somewhat less attention. This relative dearth of research is unexpected, considering one of the main criticisms of conservatism during the same period: its perceived negative impact on information usefulness for stock market participants, particularly in equity valuation (Kothari et al., 2010).

Indeed, in a literature survey published toward the end of the 2000s, Armstrong et al. (2010, p. 190) noted that "the potential for conservative accounting to assist investors in valuation is an interesting area for future research, given the common perception (or, possibly, misperception) that although conservative accounting may assist firms in contracting and governance settings, such benefits come at the expense of accounting's role in valuation." Additionally, in another survey paper from the same year, Dechow et al. (2010) found no articles they would classify as studies on the consequences of asymmetric reporting timeliness on the equity market. However, accounting researchers did not ignore the call for research on conservatism and the stock market, as the subsequent sections of this chapter will illustrate.

4.2 The Stock Market as a Determinant of Conservatism

4.2.1 Conservatism in Public and Private Firms

The research discussed in the preceding section supports the idea that lenders both demand and benefit from conservatism. However, it does not directly explore whether a similar demand exists from (or if comparable benefits can be derived by) stock market investors. An associated research question concerns whether the supply of (and demand for) conservatism varies between private firms and publicly traded firms.

Several papers have tackled this question. For instance, Ball and Shivakumar (2005) examined UK private and public companies subject to similar financial reporting, auditing, and taxation regulations. Despite these similarities, they argued that private companies report losses less promptly due to a lack of market demand for conservatism. Their empirical findings supported this argument.

Looking at financial institutions, Craig Nichols et al. (2008) found that public banks exhibit stronger levels of conservatism by recognizing earnings declines more promptly, earnings increases less promptly, and larger and timelier loan losses. In a subsequent study, Givoly et al. (2010) discovered that public companies are more likely to engage in earnings management practices and have lower accrual quality. However, they also found evidence suggesting that public companies demonstrate higher levels of conservatism, which the authors attribute to greater litigation risk and agency costs experienced by public firms. However, Peek et al. (2010) argued that the heightened conservatism observed among public firms relative to private firms stems from creditors' demand for asymmetric timeliness rather than investors' demand. They conducted a study across various countries and found that the disparity in asymmetric timeliness between public and private firms increases with a country's degree of creditor protection but not with its level of investor protection.

Thus, the literature exploring differences in conservatism between public and private firms has provided evidence consistent with a stronger demand for conservatism from the stakeholders of public firms. However, it has not conclusively answered whether this demand originates from stock market investors rather than other stakeholders.

4.2.2 The Information Role of Conservatism in the Stock Market

One of the earliest and most notable studies to directly investigate whether conservatism can stem from the demand of (and provide benefits to) equity investors is LaFond and Watts (2008). They observed that prior research suggested conservatism's existence across countries was tied to financial statements' roles in contracting, litigation, political processes, and taxation. However, they argued that "agency costs generated by the manager's private information and asymmetric loss function are not limited to debt and compensation contracts" (p. 447). LaFond and Watts (2008) proposed that conservatism mitigates managers' incentives and ability to manipulate earnings, thus benefiting equity investors by reducing information asymmetry and its associated losses. In other words, they suggested that conservatism is a corporate governance mechanism that enhances shareholder value. Their findings supported this argument, indicating that higher information asymmetry is associated with greater conservatism. Moreover, they showed that changes in information asymmetry lead to corresponding changes in conservatism, confirming a causal relationship between the two.

Subsequently, Khan and Watts (2009) further bolstered the arguments advanced by LaFond and Watts (2008). Employing an event-study framework, they showed that conservatism increases following significant rises in bid/ask spread and return volatility. This supported the notion that conservatism emerges in response to uncertainty and information asymmetry in the stock market.

4.2.3 What Type of Investors Demand Conservatism?

By the beginning of the second decade of the century, Ramalingegowda and Yu (2012, p. 98) noted that "recent research suggesting that shareholders demand conservative financial reporting raises the question: Which shareholders demand conservatism?". They argued that individual investors are unlikely to be sophisticated enough to assess a firm's conservatism level and generate demand for it. By contrast, institutional investors have, on the one hand, the resources and the sophistication to create such a demand and, on the other hand, the knowledge to understand the benefits of conservatism. Consistent with this argument, they found a positive association between institutional ownership and conservatism. Interestingly, they found the association stronger when growth options and information asymmetry are higher. This further corroborated the argument developed by LaFond and Watts (2008) and Khan and Watts (2009) that stock market investors' demand for conservatism is linked to the information benefits that conservatism can provide in the presence of uncertainty and information asymmetry.

An earlier study examining the association between conservatism and a specific type of ownership is LaFond and Roychowdhury (2008), who investigated whether managerial ownership is associated with conservatism. They argued that if conservatism is a corporate governance mechanism to address agency problems arising from the separation of ownership (i.e., equity investors) and control (i.e., managers), managerial ownership should be associated with lower conservatism. Their argument is based on the following line of thought. When managerial ownership is high, the alignment between the interests of managers and other shareholders increases, and, therefore, agency conflicts are attenuated. As a result, the shareholders' demand for conservatism becomes weaker. Consistent with this argument, they found that the asymmetric timeliness of earnings declines with managerial ownership.

A later study by Chen et al. (2014) is related to this stream of literature. They examined the relationship between conservatism and the type of ownership in the context of family-controlled businesses. They argued that family ownership is characterized by long investment horizon and large, under-diversified equity stake. Consequently, family owners have the incentives and the ability to implement conservatism in financial reports to reduce legal liability and attenuate agency conflicts with other stakeholders. Consistent with their argument, they found that conservatism increases with non-CEO family ownership.

A more recent paper examining conservatism among family firms is by Raithatha and Shaw (2019). They focused on whether family members' involvement in the firm's management and affiliation to a business group are drivers of conservatism. They found that conservatism is higher among family-controlled firms, mainly when family members manage the firm and are affiliated with a business group.

4.3 Conservatism Consequences for the Stock Market

4.3.1 Evidence of Beneficial Effects

Central to many of the papers discussed above is the argument that stock market investors demand conservatism because of the information benefits that conservatism provides. A study directly investigating whether conservatism has informational benefits to shareholders is Kim and Pevzner (2010). They found evidence that higher conservatism in current periods reduces the future likelihood of the firm missing analyst forecasts, reporting earnings decreases, and announcing dividend decreases. They also found some evidence that the stock market reacts stronger (weaker) to good (bad) earnings news of more conservative firms, suggesting that investors understand and appreciate the information benefits of conservatism.

Aligning with Kim and Pevzner's (2010) findings, Kim and Zhang (2016) examined whether conservatism is associated with the risk of future price crashes. They argued that timely recognition of losses impairs managers' ability to let bad news accumulate unreported for long periods, thus mitigating the likelihood that the sudden revelation of large amounts of previously undisclosed bad news leads to price crashes. Consistently, they found a negative association between conservatism and future price crash likelihood. Interestingly, they found the effect stronger among firms characterized by higher information asymmetry, which also corroborates the link between conservatism and stock market investors' benefits hypothesized by LaFond and Watts (2008) and Khan and Watts (2009).

Adopting an event-study approach, Kim et al. (2013) found that issuers with more conservatism experience fewer adverse market reactions to seasoned equity offerings (SEO) announcements. Importantly, they further showed that conservatism is associated with SEO announcement returns by attenuating the impact of information asymmetry.

Other studies explored the benefits of conservatism around significant events. For instance, D'Augusta et al. (2016) showed that conservatism reduces investor disagreement around earnings announcements. Also consistent with conservatism's effect on investor disagreement, Mashruwala and Mashruwala (2018) discovered that conservatism contributes to enhancing market efficiency by offsetting the inclination toward overvaluation arising from investor opinion divergence combined with short-selling constraints. Shifting the focus from earnings announcements to management forecasts, D'Augusta (2022) argued that conservatism improves the credibility of earnings guidance. Consistent with this argument, he reported that conservatism is associated with a more favorable market reaction to the release of positive forecasts and smaller investor uncertainty around the issuance of negative guidance.

While the papers discussed above have examined investor appreciation of conservatism's benefits by looking at their reaction to earnings news in an event-study framework, other papers investigated a different aspect, namely whether such benefits result in a lower cost of equity capital. Examining the association between the cost of equity and various earnings properties, Francis et al. (2004) found that conservatism is an earnings attribute not strongly associated with the cost of equity. However, a later study by Garcìa Lara et al. (2011) reported a significant negative association between conservatism and excess average stock returns from 1975 to 2003, consistent with conservatism reducing the cost of equity. In a more recent paper, Li (2015) studied the consequence of conservatism on the cost of capital at the international level, finding that the equity and debt capital costs are lower in countries with more conservative financial reporting systems and that this association more pronounced in countries with stronger legal enforcement.

Other aspects of the positive information consequences of conservatism in the stock market were explored by Garcìa Lara et al. (2014). Specifically, they tested whether conservatism leads to a future reduction in information asymmetry. Consistently, they found that increases in conservatism lead to a decrease in the bid-ask spread and stock return volatility, to more precise and less dispersed analyst forecasts, and more analysts following the firm. Garcia Lara et al.'s (2014) findings are consistent with earlier evidence by Sohn (2012), who analyzed the association between conservatism and analyst forecast error and found that forecasting earnings is easier for more conservative firms and that analysts are able to incorporate conservatism into their earnings forecasts.

4.3.2 *Evidence of Adverse Effects*

As discussed in Chap. 2, many of the arguments that led to criticism toward conservatism were motivated by the notion that conservatism would have adverse information consequences for shareholders, particularly concerning their information needs for valuation purposes. Indeed, various studies have found evidence of such detrimental effects.

For instance, Penman and Zhang (2002) explored how a company's conservative accounting practices and investment changes jointly influence earnings quality. They argue that when investments grow, reported earnings decrease while reserves increase, while the opposite happens when investments decline. If such changes are temporary, current earnings may not accurately reflect future earnings. While Penman and Zhang's (2002) study focused on unconditional conservatism proxies, the findings suggest investors may overlook how conservatism and investment changes affect reported earnings quality. In a similar vein, Mensah et al. (2004) argued that "since conservatism can be viewed as a timing issue, with bad news reflected in earnings earlier than good news, one likely effect of increased conservatism is that earnings are likely to be more volatile under conservatism than under neutral (unbiased) accounting" (p. 161). Since higher volatility can be expected to be associated with higher forecast dispersion and error, they hypothesized and found that these two analyst uncertainty metrics are positively associated with unconditional conservatism proxies.

More recently, Barth et al. (2020) argued that asymmetric recognition timeliness of good and bad news adds complexity to interpreting the earnings signal for investment decisions. Therefore, they hypothesized that conservatism is associated with a slower resolution of investor disagreement and uncertainty around earnings announcements. Consistent with the view that users may struggle with interpreting the implications of conservative earnings for future earnings, D'Augusta and Redigolo (2019) found that analysts can benefit from early-released management guidance to unravel the effects of conservatism on the earnings time series.

Another paper related to whether the stock market understands the time-series implications of earnings conservatism is Narayanamoorthy (2006), who examined the stock market consequences of conservatism-induced volatility in the post-earnings announcement drift (PEAD) context. Since the PEAD results from investors' failure to understand earnings persistence and since bad news is less persistent due to conservatism, the PEAD should be smaller for bad news than good news. Consistent with this argument, Narayanamoorthy (2006) provided "evidence the market, in forming earnings expectations, ignores the time-series properties of earnings due to accounting conservatism" (p. 764).

Other studies have documented the adverse effects of conservatism on valuation. For instance, Chen et al. (2014) showed that the reduction of earnings persistence driven by the timely recognition of bad news dominated the increase in persistence caused by the gradual recognition of good news. Therefore, an overall negative association between conservatism and persistence can emerge. Analyzing the stock market consequences of conservatism by looking at pricing multiples, they found that investors tend to discount earnings reported more conservatively. While they acknowledged "the benefits of conservatism stemming from contracting efficiencies, mitigation of litigation risk or reductions in information asymmetry," their findings documented "that such benefits are outweighed by a potential cost from conservative reporting choices in that pricing multiples are lower for conservative firms." (p. 236).

Also focusing on the pricing implications of conservatism, Kim et al. (2019) investigated whether financial analysts grasp the valuation implications of unconditional conservatism when predicting target prices. They argued that, although conservatism influences reported earnings, it does not directly impact the present value of future cash flows. They found that analysts often neglect to adjust for conservatism in their earnings forecasts, resulting in biased target prices. Moreover, they found that more experienced analysts tend to adjust for conservatism more effectively. Their evidence underscored analysts' potential oversight of conservative accounting's valuation effects, hampering market pricing efficiency.

The study by Heflin et al. (2015) also focused on conservatism's effects on earnings persistence and the related valuation implications. They analyzed whether conservatism in GAAP earnings leads users to utilize non-GAAP performance measures (i.e., "street" earnings). They found that conservatism lowers the persistence and informativeness of GAAP earnings, which in turn impairs analysts' ability to forecast such earnings. Consequently, when conservatism is higher, analysts' adjustments to GAAP earnings make street earnings a more useful signal to investors.

4.4 Conservatism and the Macroeconomic Environment

Accounting research has analyzed time-series variations in conservatism, finding that conservatism has increased over time (Givoly & Hayn, 2000). There is some evidence that part of this increase may have been due to regulatory shock and corporate scandals. For instance, Krishnan (2007) found that conservatism increased in 2002 for former Arthur Andersen clients, suggesting that auditors and managers see conservatism as a risk management strategy in the wake of significant accounting fraud cases. Also, Lobo and Zhou (2010) found that the Sarbanes–Oxley Act (SOX) resulted in higher conditional and unconditional conservatism among public firms, especially for those most aggressive in the pre-SOX period.

Various other studies have investigated whether macroeconomic factors affect firms' propensity to report conservatively. In particular, separate streams of research can be identified that analyzed the relationship between conservatism and investor sentiment, periods of crisis, or macroeconomic uncertainty.

4.4.1 Investor Sentiment

Various studies have investigated whether investor sentiment, defined as optimism or pessimism about stocks not supported by firm fundamentals (Baker & Wurgler, 2006, 2007), affects whether earnings are reported aggressively or conservatively. Analyzing abnormal accruals, some papers have found evidence of managers' aggressive reporting behavior during periods of strong sentiment. For instance, Rajgopal et al. (2007) suggested managers cater to investors by inflating earnings when investors are more optimistic about earnings news. Vice versa, when investors are pessimistic, managers rely on income-decreasing accruals and report more conservatively, "which may be partly due to increased worries about potential litigation related to financial reporting" (p. 4). Consistent with Rajgopal et al. (2007), Ali and Gurun (2009) found that managers manipulate earnings upwards during periods of high market sentiment. Similarly, Simpson (2013) reported that managers inflate earnings in periods of higher sentiment but report more conservatively during low sentiment periods. Additionally, André et al. (2016) showed that the 2008–09 crisis led U.S. firms to recognize goodwill impairments more timely than European counterparts.

However, looking at earnings asymmetric timeliness measures, Ge et al. (2019) argued that stock price overvaluation in times of strong market sentiment can increase litigation risk, inducing managers to report more conservatively. Similarly, Duong et al. (2018) argued that managers prefer to anticipate losses to release bad news during high sentiment periods rather than later.

4.4.2 Market Crises

Some studies found evidence of higher conservatism following crisis periods or during economic contractions. For instance, Jenkins et al. (2009) suggested that a greater focus on downside risk prompts management and auditors to adopt more conservative reporting in economic downturns. They offered three reasons: Firstly, recessionary periods increase the risk of litigation due to sharp stock market declines. Secondly, investors seek more conservative accounting amid economic uncertainty. Lastly, with internal funding constrained during downturns, firms may rely more on external financing, necessitating reduced information asymmetry and, thus, more conservative accounting.

Similarly, Chen et al. (2016) studied U.S. public banks before, during, and after the 2008–09 financial crisis. They found that during the crisis, there was a clear link between auditors' involvement, shown by higher audit fees, and conservative financial reporting, particularly in discretionary loan loss provisions. However, this link weakened after the crisis.

Also focusing on the financial sector, Han et al. (2018) showed that insurers tended to provide more conservative reserve estimates during the 2008–2009 financial crisis. They interpreted this trend as a possible response to the heightened threat of litigation and regulatory scrutiny during such turbulent periods, suggesting firms may adopt a more cautious approach to reporting loss reserves. Another study investigating conservatism in the financial industry amid a crisis is Manganaris et al. (2017), who reported a significant increase in conservatism levels after the 2008 crisis, evident in timelier loan loss provisions, timelier recognition of bad news, and negative accruals. Additionally, they found higher timeliness following the crisis's onset. These findings can be interpreted as banks' attempts to enhance transparency post-crisis, aiming to mitigate the adverse effects of the industry's typical opacity.

Kousenidis et al. (2013) investigated the impact of the European Debt crisis in 2011 on the earnings quality of listed firms in countries with weak fiscal sustainability (Spain, Greece, Ireland, Italy, and Portugal). They reported that firms with stronger earnings management incentives demonstrated a slower recognition of negative news in their earnings during the crisis, consistent with reduced conservatism. Other studies, however, showed that country-specific institutional factors can lower conservatism during economic turbulence. For instance, Persakis and Iatridis (2015) found that during the 2008 crisis, earnings quality and conservatism deteriorated in countries without strong shareholder protection.

While the papers discussed above focused on whether conservatism increases during and after crisis periods, a different but related research question concerns how conservatism affects the firm information environment in such periods. This question has become more pressing over the last 15 years, which have witnessed two unprecedented global crises in modern times, i.e., the 2008 financial crisis and the Covid-19 pandemic, that deeply affected stock market valuations and investor processing of financial information. These two macroeconomic shocks provided an excellent setting to study conservatism's information effects in situations of heightened uncertainty.

Focusing on the 2008 crisis, Francis et al. (2013) analyzed the impact of conservative accounting on shareholder value. They found a positive correlation between conservatism and firm stock performance, particularly for firms with weaker corporate governance or higher information asymmetry. This supported the argument that conservatism serves as an efficient governance mechanism, mitigating information risk and benefiting shareholders during market turmoil.

Balakrishnan et al. (2016) investigated the impact of conservatism on firm investment during the 2007–2008 financial crisis. Their findings were consistent with conservatism mitigating underinvestment amid information uncertainties. Specifically, they showed that firms with less conservative financial reporting experienced steeper investment declines post-crisis, especially if financially constrained or facing higher information asymmetry. Conversely, more conservative firms saw lesser declines in debt-raising and stock performance.

Also analyzing conservatism's effect on a firm's borrowing capacity during a crisis, Zhang (2020) found a positive association between conditional conservatism and access to trade credit before and after 2008, reflecting suppliers' preference for conservatism. However, they also observed the effect weaker after the crisis, especially in contexts of low information asymmetry and strong customer bargaining power, suggesting that liquid suppliers are more lenient toward less conservative customers. More recently, Kim and Shawn (2022) aligned with these findings, reporting that firms were more conservative during the 2008 financial crisis and experienced better post-crisis performance.

Focusing instead on the Covid-19 crisis, Cui et al. (2021) found that Chinese firms with greater conservatism experienced a smaller decline in stock returns, especially in the presence of greater post-Covid-19 information asymmetry. These results reinforced the notion that conservatism provided significant information benefits during the pandemic, aiding stock return valuation. Similarly, D'Augusta and Grossetti (2023) examined investor reaction to earnings news as the pandemic unraveled in early 2020. They found evidence of higher volatility and worse stock return performance, consistent with Covid causing investors to struggle with pricing the news. However, firms with a prior reputation for conservative accounting were less affected by Covid-induced uncertainty.

4.4.3 Macroeconomic Uncertainty

A separate but related stream of research analyzes different aspects of macroeconomic uncertainty and their effect on conservatism. For instance, Dai and Ngo (2021) analyzed political uncertainty and argued that such uncertainty amplifies information asymmetry, leading to heightened demand for conservatism. Consistent with this prediction, analyzing U.S. gubernatorial election cycles from 1963 to 2016, they observed increased asymmetric news recognition during periods of political uncertainty. They reported this effect as stronger for firms in states with lower electoral participation, greater industry exposure to contracting needs, higher leverage, lower managerial ownership, and stronger internal corporate governance.

Cui et al. (2023) focused on "uncertainty of uncertainty" (UOU), which they define as uncertainty that cannot be described by a certain probability measure and is also referred to as Knightian uncertainty or ambiguity in the literature. They argued that contract demand is a primary driver of the association between conservatism and UOU since UOU exacerbates manager–creditor information asymmetry, driving creditors to demand greater conservatism. Consistent with this intuition, they found that conservatism is positively associated with UOU, proxied by the volatility of economic policy uncertainty.

Related to these findings, although not examining conservatism's relationship with time-varying uncertainty, Hsieh et al. (2019) studied the relationship between conservatism and the ambiguity stemming from the business strategy pursued by the firm. They argued that firms employing prospector strategies face greater ambiguity by actively seeking new business opportunities than firms employing defender strategies, which focus on utilizing existing resources. They found that the former strategy is associated with greater conservatism, consistent with a positive link between conservatism and ambiguity.

4.4.4 Managers' Behavioral Traits

Studies examining managers' optimism and confidence shed further light on the relationship between the macroeconomic environment and conservatism, as the economic outlook often influences these behavioral traits. For instance, Ahmed and Duellman (2013) contended that managers who exhibit overconfidence tend to overestimate future cash flows obtainable from their firms' investments and, therefore, will postpone recognizing losses and employ less conservative accounting practices. Their analysis, incorporating conditional and unconditional conservatism measures, consistently revealed a negative correlation between CEO overconfidence and conservatism. Additionally, they noted that external monitoring mechanisms, proxied by CEO duality, did not seem to alleviate this tendency.

Similarly, Collins et al. (2024) analyzed the association of conservatism with manager sentiment, which refers to widely held beliefs held by financial managers concerning the future economic prospects of their firms that are not supported by available economic data. They posited that managerial sentiment will likely influence conditional conservative reporting since the decision to recognize unrealized economic losses promptly stems from financial managers' perceptions of their firms' future cash flow prospects. Their findings consistently supported that manager sentiment is inversely related to conditional conservatism. This suggests that firms tend to adopt less conservative reporting practices during periods characterized by high managerial sentiment, indicative of over-optimism while opting for more conservative practices during periods of low manager sentiment, suggestive of over-pessimism.

4.5 Stock Market Information Effects of Conservatism vs. Voluntary Disclosures

Financial statements are one of the primary avenues through which stock market investors gain insights into a firm's fundamentals. In addition to financial statements, firms employ various voluntary disclosure channels—including management forecasts, press releases, conference calls, and narrative disclosures like the Management Discussion and Analysis—to disseminate similar information to the markets. Extensive research has explored the association between conservatism and voluntary disclosure practices, investigating this relationship empirically and analytically.

In a theoretical paper, Gigler and Hemmer (2001) argued that as a firm's financial reporting system adopts greater conservatism, the risk-sharing benefits of timely disclosure diminish, reducing the value of preemptive voluntary disclosures. Consequently, they posited that higher conservatism diminishes firms' likelihood of releasing timely voluntary disclosures. Another theoretical study by Langberg and Sivaramakrishnan (2008) demonstrated that conservative accounting systems may lead to more frequent but less conservative voluntary disclosures in equilibrium. Specifically, they observed a lower threshold quality level for disclosing hard information to the public within conservative accounting systems. Conversely, under aggressive accounting systems, voluntary disclosures are less frequent and more conservative. Langberg and Sivaramakrishnan (2008) interpreted these findings as a cautionary note that conservatism in mandatory financial reporting may inadvertently affect voluntary disclosure practices.

One of the first empirical papers examining the relationship between conservatism and voluntary disclosures is by Hui et al. (2009). They argued that conservatism is a substitute for management forecasts, thereby reducing information asymmetry in the market and mitigating potential litigation risks through prompt reporting of negative news. Their findings revealed a negative association between unconditional conservatism proxies and management forecasts' frequency, specificity, and timeliness. More recently, Jaggi et al. (2021) revisited Hui et al. (2009), employing the methodology developed by Li et al. (2016) to differentiate between cost of capital management forecasts, disclose or abstain forecasts, and opportunistic forecasts. They found that while conservatism substitutes for the first type of forecast, it does not for the other two types.

Furthermore, other studies have uncovered evidence of substitutive effects between conservatism and forms of disclosures other than earnings guidance. For example, D'Augusta and DeAngelis (2020b) showed that when earnings are less conservative, the Management's Discussion and Analysis (MD&A) tone is more reactive to bad earnings news but less responsive to good earnings news. They interpreted these findings as indicating that when earnings are more conservative, managers are more confident in their ability to sustain positive performance and, consequently, less inclined to downplay good earnings news. Additionally, Cho et al. (2020) found that firms with conservative financial reporting are less likely to disclose CSR information, and the market's reaction to CSR disclosures diminishes with increased financial reporting conservatism.

Conversely, several studies have underscored that the relationship between conservatism and voluntary disclosures extends beyond substitutive effects to include complementarities. For instance, an analytical study by Guay and Verrecchia (2018) contended that in the absence of mandatory disclosure requirements, managers tend to selectively disclose positive outcomes while concealing negative ones. This managerial inclination toward disclosing good news, complemented by a financial reporting system mandating timely disclosure of bad news, can reduce uncertainty and enhance firm value. Supporting this notion, D'Augusta and Redigolo (2019) found that higher conservatism in current earnings is associated with an increased likelihood of "early" earnings guidance, particularly when such guidance predicts positive earnings trends. They also observe analysts utilizing this guidance to update their forecasts, indicating its relevance.

Examining the narrative aspect of disclosures, D'Augusta and DeAngelis (2020a) proposed that conservatism hinders managers' ability to manipulate the tone of disclosures, making it difficult to downplay bad news and exaggerate good news. Their findings show a negative association between upward tone management in the Management's Discussion and Analysis section of 10-K and conservatism, especially in firms where incentives for tone manipulation are high. Moreover, they show that conservatism neither fosters downward tone management nor inhibits the conveyance of genuine future good news, underscoring its role in enhancing disclosure narratives.

In conclusion, research indicates a complex and multifaceted relationship between conservatism and voluntary disclosures, both concerning firms' decisions to make such disclosures and investors' reactions to them. The studies discussed above highlight that while conservatism may substitute for certain disclosure practices, it can also play a complementary role in other settings, ultimately influencing market perceptions and firm value.

4.6 Conservatism and the Stock Market: International Evidence

Paralleling researchers' efforts to better understand conservatism's relationship with the stock market within the U.S. setting, the recent decades have witnessed increased attention to addressing such research questions at the international level. Such investigation is crucial not solely for replication purposes but also due to significant legal, institutional, and cultural differences that can profoundly influence how conservative reporting practices in companies are shaped by capital market forces and how these practices impact economic outcomes for investors. These factors emphasize the need for targeted studies to understand conservatism's relationship with the stock market beyond the borders of the USA.

Among the first studies to address such a need, Ball et al. (2000) suggested that the market demand for timelier recognition of losses is stronger in common law countries than in code law countries. They argued that the two types of countries are characterized by corporate governance models that differ in how they resolve information asymmetry (public disclosure vs. private communication). Consistently, they found conservatism stronger in common law countries than code law countries, although all countries show a certain degree of conservatism. However, analyzing the East Asian countries—Hong Kong, Malaysia, Singapore, and Thailand—Ball et al. (2003) suggested that accounting standards that derive from common-law sources do not necessarily imply higher conservatism because of the critical role played by managerial incentives in conditioning the supply of high-quality financial reports. Shedding further light on the role played by incentives in determining the differences in conservatism across countries, Bushman and Piotroski (2006) examined how countries' features, such as the judicial system and the enforcement of securities laws, influence the behavior of executives and stakeholders and therefore affect conservatism. They showed that the recognition of losses is timelier in countries with strong investor protections and high-quality judicial systems.

Pope and Walker (1999) analyzed differences in recognition timeliness and conservatism between the USA and the UK. They showed that Ball et al. (2000) conclusions about the differences in conservatism between the USA and the UK "are sensitive both to the measurement of conservatism and to the components of earnings examined." (p. 54). Specifically, they showed that earnings before extraordinary items appear more conservative in the USA and earnings after extraordinary items are more conservative in the UK. They interpreted their results to "suggest that U.K. firms recognize bad news faster than U.S. firms, but that they classify the bad news differently" (p. 55). In a later paper, Ball et al. (2008) exploited the international research setting to address whether conservatism stems from the demand of the stock market or debt market participants. Analyzing annual earnings observations from 22 countries, they found evidence that accounting earnings properties such as timeliness and conservatism are more likely driven by debt rather than the stock market.

While the studies discussed above examine the capital markets' demand for conservatism in the international setting, others have delved into conservatism's effects, especially in connection with shareholders' information needs for valuation purposes. For instance, Brown et al. (2006) investigated whether conservatism impacts the value relevance of earnings in an international context. They found that conservatism increases relevance in countries with high accrual intensity. They interpreted these findings to support the notion that conservatism serves "as an efficient contracting role to reduce managers' opportunistic behavior in the use of accruals" (p. 605). Another paper studying the association between conservatism and the value relevance of earnings in a non-U.S. setting is by Kousenidis et al. (2009). Exploring the Greek market, they found a non-linear association between conservatism and earnings value relevance; specifically, value relevance increases when moving from low- to medium-conservative levels but decreases when moving to high levels.

Other studies focused on global crises to enrich the picture provided in Sect. 4.4 with international evidence. For instance, Herrmann et al. (2008) found a significant increase in conservatism following the Asian financial crisis in Thailand. Additionally, they reported that Big Four audit clients demonstrated greater sensitivity to bad news than non-Big Four audit clients, particularly during the crisis period. At the same time, both Big Four and non-Big Four audit clients report more conservative earnings in the post-crisis period. Another study investigating the levels of conservatism and timeliness of earnings during the period surrounding the 1997 Asian financial crisis is Vichitsarawong et al. (2010), who examined the Hong Kong, Malaysia, Singapore, and Thailand markets. Their findings revealed that both conservatism and the timeliness of earnings improved in the post-crisis period, surpassing even the levels observed in the pre-crisis period.

References

Ahmed, A. S., Billings, B. K., Morton, R. M., & Stanford-Harris, M. (2002). The role of accounting conservatism in mitigating bondholder-shareholder conflicts over dividend policy and in reducing debt costs. *The Accounting Review, 77*(4), 867–890.

Ahmed, A. S., & Duellman, S. (2007). Accounting conservatism and board of director characteristics: An empirical analysis. *Journal of Accounting and Economics, 43*(2–3), 411–437.

Ahmed, A. S., & Duellman, S. (2013). Managerial overconfidence and accounting conservatism. *Journal of Accounting Research, 51*(1), 1–30.

Ali, A., & Gurun, U. G. (2009). Investor sentiment, accruals anomaly, and accruals management. *Journal of Accounting, Auditing & Finance, 24*(3), 415–431.

André, P., Filip, A., & Paugam, L. (2016). Examining the patterns of goodwill impairments in Europe and the US. *Accounting in Europe, 13*(3), 329–352.

Armstrong, C. S., Guay, W. R., & Weber, J. P. (2010). The role of information and financial reporting in corporate governance and debt contracting. *Journal of Accounting and Economics, 50*(2–3), 179–234.

Baker, M. P., & Wurgler, J. (2006). Investor sentiment and the cross-section of stock returns. *Journal of Finance, 61*(4), 1645–1680.

Baker, M. P., & Wurgler, J. (2007). Investor sentiment in the stock market. *Journal of Economic Perspectives, 21*(2), 129–151.

Balakrishnan, K., Watts, R. L., & Zuo, L. (2016). The effect of accounting conservatism on corporate investment during the global financial crisis. *Journal of Business Finance & Accounting, 43*(5 & 6), 513–542.

Ball, R., Kothari, S. P., & Robin, A. (2000). The effect of international institutional factors on properties of accounting earnings. *Journal of Accounting and Economics, 29*, 1–51.

Ball, R., Robin, A., & Sadka, G. (2008). Is financial reporting shaped by equity markets or by debt markets? An international study of timeliness and conservatism. *Review of Accounting Studies, 13*(2–3), 168–205.

Ball, R., Robin, A., & Wu, J. S. (2003). Incentives versus standards: Properties of accounting income in four East Asian countries. *Journal of Accounting and Economics, 36*(1–3), 235–270.

Ball, R., & Shivakumar, L. (2005). Earnings quality in UK private firms: Comparative loss recognition timeliness. *Journal of Accounting and Economics, 39*(1), 83–128.

Barth, M. E., Landsman, W. R., Raval, V., & Wang, S. (2020). Asymmetric timeliness and the resolution of investor disagreement and uncertainty at earnings announcements. *The Accounting Review, 95*(4), 23–50.

Basu, S. (1997). The conservatism principle and the asymmetric timeliness of earnings. *Journal of Accounting and Economics, 24*(1), 3–37.

Beatty, A. L., Weber, J. P., & Yu, J. J. (2008). Conservatism and debt. *Journal of Accounting and Economics, 45*(2–3), 154–174.

Beaver, W. H., & Ryan, S. G. (2005). Conditional and unconditional conservatism: Concepts and modeling. *Review of Accounting Studies, 10*(2–3), 269–309.

Beekes, W., Pope, P. F., & Young, S. (2004). The link between earnings timeliness, earnings conservatism and board composition: Evidence from the UK. *Corporate Governance, 12*(1), 47–59.

Brown, W. D., He, H., & Teitel, K. (2006). Conditional conservatism and the value relevance of accounting earnings: An international study. *European Accounting Review, 15*(4), 605–626.

Bushman, R. M., & Piotroski, J. D. (2006). Financial reporting incentives for conservative accounting: The influence of legal and political institutions. *Journal of Accounting and Economics, 42*(1–2), 107–148.

Cameran, M., Prencipe, A., & Trombetta, M. (2016). Mandatory audit firm rotation and audit quality. *European Accounting Review, 25*(1), 35–58.

Cano-Rodríguez, M. (2010). Big auditors, private firms and accounting conservatism: Spanish evidence. *European Accounting Review, 19*(1), 131–159.

Chen, L. H., Folsom, D., Paek, W., & Sami, H. (2014). Accounting conservatism, earnings persistence and pricing multiples on earnings. *Accounting Horizons, 28*(2), 233–260.

Chen, F., Lam, K., Smieliauskas, W., & Ye, M. (2016). Auditor conservatism and banks' measurement uncertainty during the financial crisis. *International Journal of Auditing, 20*(1), 52–65.

Cho, S. Y., Kang, P. K., Lee, C., & Park, C. (2020). Financial reporting conservatism and voluntary CSR disclosure. *Accounting Horizons, 34*(2), 63–82.

Chung, R., Firth, M., & Kim, J.-B. (2003). Auditor conservatism and reported earnings. *Accounting and Business Research, 33*(1), 19–32.

Collins, D. W., Nguyen, N. Q., & Nguyen, T. T. (2024). Manager sentiment and conditional conservatism. *Journal of Business Finance & Accounting*.

Craig Nichols, D., Wahlen, J. M., & Wieland, M. M. (2008). Publicly traded versus privately held: Implications for conditional conservatism in bank accounting. *Review of Accounting Studies, 14*(1), 88–122.

Cui, L., Kent, P., Kim, S., & Li, S. (2021). Accounting conservatism and firm performance during the COVID-19 pandemic. *Accounting & Finance, 61*(4), 5543–5579.

Cui, X., Ma, T., Xie, X., & Goodell, J. W. (2023). Uncertainty of uncertainty and accounting conservatism. *Finance Research Letters, 52*, 103525.

D'Augusta, C. (2022). Does accounting conservatism make good news forecasts more credible and bad news forecasts less alarming? *Journal of Accounting, Auditing & Finance, 37*(1), 77–113.

D'Augusta, C., Bar-Yosef, S., & Prencipe, A. (2016). The effects of conservative reporting on investor disagreement. *European Accounting Review, 25*(3), 451–485.

D'Augusta, C., & DeAngelis, M. D. (2020a). Does accounting conservatism discipline qualitative disclosure? Evidence from tone management in the MD&A. *Contemporary Accounting Research, 37*(4), 2287–2318.

D'Augusta, C., & DeAngelis, M. D. (2020b). Tone concavity around expected earnings. *The Accounting Review, 95*(1), 133–164.

D'Augusta, C., & Grossetti, F. (2023). How did Covid-19 affect investors' interpretation of earnings news? The role of accounting conservatism. *Finance Research Letters, 52*, 103504.

D'Augusta, C., & Redigolo, G. (2019). Do firms use early guidance to disclose the effect of conservatism on future earnings? *Review of Accounting and Finance, 18*(3), 432–455.

Dai, L., & Ngo, P. (2021). Political uncertainty and accounting conservatism. *European Accounting Review, 30*(2), 277–307.

Dechow, P. M., Ge, W., & Schrand, C. M. (2010). Understanding earnings quality: A review of the proxies, their determinants and their consequences. *Journal of Accounting and Economics, 50*, 344–401.

Duong, H. K., Schuldt, M., & Gotti, G. (2018). Investor sentiment and timely loss recognition. *Review of Accounting and Finance, 17*(3), 383–404.

Francis, B., Hasan, I., & Wu, Q. (2013). The benefits of conservative accounting to shareholders: Evidence from the financial crisis. *Accounting Horizons, 27*(2), 319–349.

Francis, J., LaFond, R., Olsson, P. M., & Schipper, K. (2004). Cost of equity and earnings attributes. *The Accounting Review, 79*(4), 967–1010.

Francis, J. R., & Wang, D. (2008). The joint effect of investor protection and big 4 audits on earnings quality around the world. *Contemporary Accounting Research, 25*(1), 157–191.

Garcìa Lara, J. M., Garcìa Osma, B., & Penalva, F. (2007). Accounting conservatism and corporate governance. *Review of Accounting Studies, 14*(1), 161–201.

Garcìa Lara, J. M., Garcìa Osma, B., & Penalva, F. (2011). Conditional conservatism and cost of capital. *Review of Accounting Studies, 16*(2), 247–271.

Garcìa Lara, J. M., Garcìa Osma, B., & Penalva, F. (2014). Information consequences of accounting conservatism. *European Accounting Review, 23*(2), 173–198.

Ge, R., Seybert, N., & Zhang, F. (2019). Investor sentiment and conditional accounting conservatism. *Accounting Horizons, 33*(1), 83–102.

Gigler, F. B., & Hemmer, T. (2001). Conservatism, optimal disclosure policy, and the timeliness of financial reports. *The Accounting Review, 76*(4), 471–493.

Gigler, F. B., Kanodia, C., Sapra, H., & Venugopalan, R. (2009). Accounting conservatism and the efficiency of debt contracts. *Journal of Accounting Research, 47*(3), 767–797.

Givoly, D., & Hayn, C. (2000). The changing time-series properties of earnings, cash flows and accruals: Has financial reporting become more conservative? *Journal of Accounting and Economics, 29*(3), 287–320.

Givoly, D., Hayn, C. K., & Katz, S. P. (2010). Does public ownership of equity improve earnings quality? *The Accounting Review, 85*(1), 195–225.

Guay, W. R., & Verrecchia, R. E. (2018). Conservative disclosure. *Journal of Financial Reporting, 3*(1), 73–92.

Han, S., Lai, G. C., & Ho, C.-L. (2018). Corporate transparency and reserve management: Evidence from US property-liability insurance companies. *Journal of Banking & Finance, 96*, 379–392.

Heflin, F., Hsu, C., & Jin, Q. (2015). Accounting conservatism and street earnings. *Review of Accounting Studies, 20*(2), 674–709.

Herrmann, D. R., Pornupatham, S., & Vichitsarawong, T. (2008). The impact of the Asian financial crisis on auditors' conservatism. *Journal of International Accounting Research, 7*(2), 43–63.

Hsieh, C. C., Ma, Z., & Novoselov, K. E. (2019). Accounting conservatism, business strategy, and ambiguity. *Accounting, Organizations and Society, 74*(643010), 41–55.

Hui, K. W., Matsunaga, S. R., & Morse, D. (2009). The impact of conservatism on management earnings forecasts. *Journal of Accounting and Economics, 47*(3), 192–207.

Jaggi, B., Ronen, J., & Xin, H. (2021). Management earnings forecast and accounting conservatism. *Journal of Accounting, Auditing & Finance, 36*(3), 451–474.

Jenkins, D. S., Kane, G. D., & Velury, U. (2009). Earnings conservatism and value relevance across the business cycle. *Journal of Business Finance & Accounting, 36*(9–10), 1041–1058.

Khan, M., & Watts, R. L. (2009). Estimation and empirical properties of a firm-year measure of accounting conservatism. *Journal of Accounting and Economics, 48*(2–3), 132–150.

Kim, Y., Li, S., Pan, C., & Zuo, L. (2013). The role of accounting conservatism in the equity market: Evidence from seasoned equity offerings. *The Accounting Review, 88*(4), 1327–1356.

Kim, J. B., Nekrasov, A., Shroff, P. K., & Simon, A. (2019). Valuation implications of unconditional accounting conservatism: Evidence from analysts' target prices. *Contemporary Accounting Research, 36*(3), 1669–1698.

Kim, B. H., & Pevzner, M. (2010). Conditional accounting conservatism and future negative surprises: An empirical investigation. *Journal of Accounting and Public Policy, 29*(4), 311–329.

Kim, T., & Shawn, H. (2022). Conservative financial reporting and resilience to the financial crisis. *Sustainability, 14*(14), Articolo 14.

Kim, J.-B., & Zhang, L. (2016). Accounting conservatism and stock price crash risk: Firm-level evidence. *Contemporary Accounting Research, 33*(1), 412–441.

Kothari, S. P., Ramanna, K., & Skinner, D. J. (2010). Implications for GAAP from an analysis of positive research in accounting. *Journal of Accounting and Economics, 50*, 246–286.

Kousenidis, D. V., Ladas, A. C., & Negakis, C. I. (2009). Value relevance of conservative and non-conservative accounting information. *The International Journal of Accounting, 44*(3), 219–238.

Kousenidis, D. V., Ladas, A. C., & Negakis, C. I. (2013). The effects of the European debt crisis on earnings quality. *International Review of Financial Analysis, 30*, 351–362.

Krishnan, G. V. (2007). Did earnings conservatism increase for former Andersen clients? *Journal of Accounting, Auditing & Finance, 22*(2), 141–163.

LaFond, R., & Roychowdhury, S. (2008). Managerial ownership and accounting conservatism. *Journal of Accounting Research, 46*(1), 101–135.

LaFond, R., & Watts, R. L. (2008). The information role of conservatism. *The Accounting Review, 83*(2), 447–478.

Langberg, N., & Sivaramakrishnan, K. (2008). Voluntary disclosures and information production by analysts. *Journal of Accounting and Economics, 46*(1), 78–100.

Li, X. (2015). Accounting conservatism and cost of capital: International analysis. *Journal of Business Finance & Accounting, 42*(5–6), 555–582.

Li, E., Wasley, C., & Zimmerman, J. (2016). The disclose or abstain incentive to issue management guidance. *Journal of Law, Finance, and Accounting, 1*(1), 187–233.

Lobo, G. J., & Zhou, J. (2010). Changes in discretionary financial reporting behavior following the Sarbanes-Oxley Act. *Journal of Accounting, Auditing & Finance, 25*(1), 1–26.

Manganaris, P., Beccalli, E., & Dimitropoulos, P. (2017). Bank transparency and the crisis. *The British Accounting Review, 49*(2), 121–137.

Mashruwala, C., & Mashruwala, S. (2018). Does accounting conservatism reduce overpricing caused by short-sales constraints? *Contemporary Accounting Research, 35*(4), 2160–2190.

Mensah, Y. M., Song, X., & Ho, S. S. M. (2004). The effect of conservatism on analysts' annual earnings forecast accuracy and dispersion. *Journal of Accounting, Auditing & Finance, 19*(2), 159–183.

Narayanamoorthy, G. S. (2006). Conservatism and cross-sectional variation in the post–earnings announcement drift. *Journal of Accounting Research, 44*(4), 763–789.

Nikolaev, V. V. (2010). Debt covenants and accounting conservatism. *Journal of Accounting Research, 48*(1), 51–89.

Peek, E., Cuijpers, R., & Buijink, W. (2010). Creditors' and shareholders' reporting demands in public versus private firms: Evidence from Europe. *Contemporary Accounting Research, 27*(1), 49–91.

Penman, S. H., & Zhang, X.-J. (2002). Accounting conservatism, the quality of earnings, and stock returns. *The Accounting Review, 77*(2), 237–264.

Persakis, A., & Iatridis, G. E. (2015). Earnings quality under financial crisis: A global empirical investigation. *Journal of Multinational Financial Management, 30*, 1–35.

Pope, P. F., & Walker, M. (1999). International differences in the timeliness, conservatism, and classification of earnings. *Journal of Accounting Research, 37*(Suppl), 53–87.

Raithatha, M., & Shaw, T. S. (2019). Do family firms choose conservative accounting practices? *International Journal of Accounting, 54*(4), 1950014.

Rajgopal, S., Shivakumar, L., & Simpson, A. (2007). A catering theory of earnings management. In *Available at SSRN 991138*.

Ramalingegowda, S., & Yu, Y. (2012). Institutional ownership and conservatism. *Journal of Accounting and Economics, 53*(1–2), 98–114.

Simpson, A. V. (2013). Does investor sentiment affect earnings management? *Journal of Business Finance & Accounting, 40*(7–8), 869–900.

Sohn, B. C. (2012). Analyst forecast, accounting conservatism and the related valuation implications. *Accounting & Finance, 52*(Suppl), 311–341.

Vichitsarawong, T., Eng, L. L., & Meek, G. K. (2010). The impact of the Asian financial crisis on conservatism and timeliness of earnings: Evidence from Hong Kong, Malaysia, Singapore, and Thailand. *Journal of International Financial Management & Accounting, 21*(1), 32–61.

Watts, R. L. (2003). Conservatism in accounting part I: Explanations and implications. *Accounting Horizons, 17*(3), 207–221.

Zhang, J. (2008). The contracting benefits of accounting conservatism to lenders and borrowers. *Journal of Accounting and Economics, 45*(1), 27–54.

Zhang, Y. (2020). Conditional conservatism and trade credit during the global financial crisis. *Journal of Accounting and Public Policy, 39*(4), 106728.

Chapter 5
Conservatism's Role in the Italian Stock Market: Three Empirical Studies

5.1 Re-examining Conservatism in the Italian Stock Market: Analysis of Determinants and Validation of Empirical Proxies

5.1.1 Motivation

The literature reviewed in Chap. 4 highlights that since the late 1990s, researchers have devoted considerable effort to examining the complex relationship between conservatism and the stock market. Much of this research has primarily focused on the U.S. context, though various studies have also analyzed how cross-country differences in regulatory and institutional settings affect conservatism's connection with the stock market.

Against this backdrop, the exploration of how conservatism interacts with capital markets in the Italian setting has received comparatively less empirical attention. This imbalance is even more noteworthy when considering the different perspectives that are specific to the Italian economic, cultural, and institutional environment, which could enrich the empirical picture painted by international literature over decades of research.

Understanding the dynamics of conservatism in the Italian context is crucial for participants in the Italian economic landscape, such as capital providers, policymakers, and practitioners, given its implications for financial reporting quality, market efficiency, and investor decision-making. It is also important to acknowledge that conclusions drawn from studies analyzing the U.S. or Asian markets cannot be seamlessly extrapolated to the Italian setting, owing to significant differences between these economic environments. Moreover, the uncritical empirical adoption of conservatism models primarily developed in the USA poses challenges.

This chapter aims to take a step forward toward filling this void in the literature by presenting three empirical studies exploring the demand for conservatism arising

C. D'Augusta, *Accounting Conservatism and the Stock Market*, SpringerBriefs in Accounting, https://doi.org/10.1007/978-3-031-67145-6_5

from the Italian capital markets and conservatism's information effects on stock market dynamics during the Covid-19 crisis. Specifically, the first study examines the robustness of alternative model specifications and compares findings with established literature on the U.S. market, thus contributing to the broader understanding of financial reporting practices and their implications in diverse market environments. Additionally, the investigation into the drivers of capital market pressures for conservatism sheds light on how market dynamics shape financial reporting practices in Italy. Furthermore, evaluating different firm-year-specific proxies of conservatism addresses the need for robust measurement tools tailored to the Italian market context, providing researchers with reliable instruments to analyze conservatism in the Italian setting.

5.1.2 Research Design

The first of the three studies presented in this chapter comprises three distinct sets of tests. Initially, I examine the level of conditional conservatism within the Italian stock market using asymmetric timeliness models based on Basu (1997). This test aims to achieve two objectives: first, to evaluate the resilience of the asymmetric timeliness coefficient estimates in alternative model specifications of the Basu (1997) conservatism model in the Italian context, and second, to compare these estimates with findings from prevalent literature on the U.S. stock market. As outlined in Chap. 3, the standard regression equation of the Basu (1997) model is represented as follows:

$$\text{EARN} = \beta 0 + \beta 1\text{RET} + \beta 2\text{NEG} + \beta 3\text{RET} * \text{NEG} + \varepsilon, \tag{5.1}$$

Here, EARN denotes net income before extraordinary items scaled by the market value of equity at the beginning of the year, RET signifies the stock market return over the year, and NEG is a binary variable identifying observations characterized by negative returns. The coefficient β3 represents the asymmetric timeliness in the recognition of good and bad news, estimating the average level of conditional conservatism within the sample under scrutiny.

Numerous studies have identified potential noise and bias affecting the original Basu (1997) model specification (Dietrich et al., 2007; Givoly et al., 2007; Patatoukas & Thomas, 2011). Subsequent research has proposed various corrections to mitigate such bias (Badia et al., 2021; Ball et al., 2013): utilizing unexpected earnings as the dependent variable, incorporating unexpected returns in the interactive explanatory variables, and including firm fixed effects in the regression equation. Therefore, I conduct the regression of Eq. (5.1), defining RET as the unexpected stock return calculated as per Badia et al. (2021) and Ball et al. (2013). Additionally, I alternately employ net income before extraordinary items scaled by the lagged market value of equity (EARN), the year-over-year change in earnings scaled by the lagged market value of equity (ΔEARN), or the unexpected earnings (Unexp. EARN) calculated following Ball et al. (2013) as dependent variables.

Moving to the second set of tests, I examine whether capital market pressures influence the extent of conditional conservatism exhibited by Italian-listed firms. This analysis, consistent with the international conservatism literature, identifies two primary drivers of capital markets' demand for conservatism: (1) the leverage ratio calculated as total liabilities divided by total assets (LEVERAGE) representing conservatism demand from the debt market and (2) stock return volatility (VOLATILITY) capturing the uncertainty and information asymmetry faced by stock market investors and, thus, their demand for timely recognition of losses.

The regression model for this analysis is formulated as:

$$\begin{aligned}\text{EARN}, \Delta\text{EARN}, \text{Unexp.EARN} &= \beta 0 + \beta 1\text{RET} + \beta 2\text{NEG} + \beta 3\text{RET} * \text{NEG} \\ &+ \beta 4\text{LEVERAGE} + \beta 5\text{LEVERAGE} * \text{RET} + \beta 6\text{LEVERAGE} * \text{NEG} \\ &+ \beta 7\text{LEVERAGE} * \text{RET} * \text{NEG} + \text{B8VOLATILITY} \\ &+ \beta 9\text{VOLATILITY} * \text{RET} + \beta 10\text{VOLATILITY} * \text{NEG} \\ &+ \beta 11\text{VOLATILITY} * \text{RET} * \text{NEG} + \text{CONTROLS} + \varepsilon\end{aligned} \tag{5.2}$$

I predict positive associations of LEVERAGE (β7) and VOLATILITY (β11) with the asymmetric timeliness coefficient. Moreover, I incorporate a vector of controls, including variables such as the logarithm of the market value of equity (SIZE), the market-to-book ratio (M/B), and the prior year value of EARN (LAG_EARN), with their interactions with RET, NEG, and RET*NEG, following the standard approach in the conservatism literature.

In the third set of tests, I evaluate the measurement validity of three different firm-year-specific proxies of conservatism widely utilized in the literature. These proxies include the Khan and Watts (2009) C-Score measure (CSCORE), the difference between the skewness of earnings and cash flows (ΔSKEWNESS) developed by Givoly and Hayn (2000), and the negative of the average value of non-operating accruals over the three prior years (Avg.Neg.Accr.) also developed by Givoly and Hayn (2000). I perform this assessment through the following regression equation:

$$\begin{aligned}\text{EARN}, \Delta\text{EARN}, \text{Unexp.EARN} &= \beta 0 + \beta 1\text{RET} + \beta 2\text{NEG} \\ &+ \beta 3\text{RET} * \text{NEG} + \beta 4\text{CONSPROXY} + \beta 5\text{CONSPROXY} * \text{RET} \\ &+ \beta 6\text{CONSPROXY} * \text{NEG} + \beta 7\text{CONSPROXY} * \text{RET} * \text{NEG} + \varepsilon\end{aligned} \tag{5.3}$$

I predict positive associations of CSCORE or ΔSKEWNESS with asymmetric timeliness, denoted by a positive coefficient β7. However, I refrain from making predictions about the sign of β7 when employing AvgNegAccr, as it captures aspects related to both conditional and unconditional conservatism, as discussed in Chap. 3.

5.1.3 Results and Discussion

The sample consists of 3136 firm-year observations for 463 Italian-listed firms from 2002 to 2022. The data are obtained from the Compustat Global database through the Wharton Research Data Services website. Descriptive statistics for the variables

Table 5.1 Descriptive statistics

	Obs.	Mean	Std. Dev.	25th perc.	Median	75th perc.
EARN	3136	0.0282	0.1085	0.0063	0.0446	0.0790
ΔEARN	3136	0.0014	0.1104	−0.0209	0.0042	0.0275
Unexp.EARN	3136	0.0073	0.0840	−0.0179	0.0088	0.0389
RET	3136	0.0297	0.3686	−0.1974	−0.0134	0.1847
SIZE	3136	5.4849	1.8759	4.0943	5.2223	6.7413
VOLATILITY	3136	0.0212	0.0078	0.0156	0.0200	0.0254
M/B	3136	2.4612	2.4396	1.0915	1.7773	2.8526
LEVERAGE	3136	0.5846	0.1804	0.4720	0.6064	0.7152
LAG_EARN	3136	0.0246	0.1092	0.0086	0.0423	0.0721
CSCORE	2974	0.0308	0.1799	−0.0803	0.0259	0.1187
ΔSKEWNESS	2386	0.0920	1.2203	−0.6330	0.0517	0.7881
Avg.Neg.Accr.	2920	0.2963	15.2100	-0.0120	0.0071	0.0290

included in the models are reported in Table 5.1, showcasing values consistent with recent conservatism literature analyzing U.S. samples (e.g., Badia et al., 2021).

Table 5.2 presents the outcomes of the initial test series (Eq. 5.1) utilizing various specifications for the dependent variable. Each specification displays two sets of coefficients: those derived from the regression estimation within the current sample (Columns 1, 3, 5, and 7) and those obtained from Ball et al. (2013) for comparative analysis (Columns 2, 4, 6, and 8). Furthermore, Columns 9 and 10 present estimates of the same specifications as in Columns 5 and 7, incorporating firm fixed effects. The results demonstrate that, regardless of the specifications used, the coefficient estimates' sign, magnitude, and significance closely correspond to expectations and are comparable to those documented by Ball et al. (2013).

These findings underscore the robustness of the Basu (1997) asymmetric timeliness model within the Italian context, exhibiting consistency across alternative specifications aimed at mitigating potential biases identified in the literature. Consequently, these results indicate that such specifications, along with their derivatives, offer a reliable means to infer conditional conservatism within the Italian stock market, comparable in reliability to studies conducted in the U.S. stock market.

Following that, Table 5.3 presents the outcomes derived from estimating Eq. (5.2). Consistent with expectations, VOLATILITY and LEVERAGE exhibit significant positive correlations with conservatism across all model specifications. These results show that similarly to findings by prior literature in the international setting, capital markets' demand for conditional conservatism can incentivize Italian-listed firms to report losses more promptly than profits.

Finally, Tables 5.4, 5.5, and 5.6 report the results from the regression Eq. 5.3. Notably, CSCORE and ΔSKEWNESS are significantly positively associated with asymmetric timeliness, thereby affirming their utility as firm-year-specific proxies for conditional conservatism within the Italian context. Conversely, as anticipated, AvgNegAccr exhibits no discernible association with asymmetric timeliness,

Table 5.2 Coefficient estimates from alternative specifications of the modified Basu (1997) model: USA vs. Italy

		EARN		EARN		ΔEARN		Unexp. EARN		ΔEARN	Unexp. EARN
		(1)	(2)	(3)	(4)	(5)	(6)	(7)	(8)	(9)	(10)
Dependent Var.:	Exp. Sign	Current sample	Ball et al. (2013)	Current sample	Ball et al. (2013)	Current sample	Ball et al. (2013)	Current sample	Ball et al. (2013)	Current sample	Current sample
RET	+	0.046***	0.020***	0.054***	0.044***	0.051***	0.059***	0.052***	0.040***	0.051***	0.051***
		(0.000)	(0.000)	(0.000)	(0.000)	(0.000)	(0.000)	(0.000)	(0.000)	(0.000)	(0.000)
NEG	+/–	0.008	0.015***	0.006	0.008***	0.010*	0.011***	0.007	0.011***	0.011	0.005
		(0.148)	(0.000)	(0.234)	(0.000)	(0.097)	(0.000)	(0.177)	(0.000)	(0.116)	(0.373)
RET*NEG	+	0.161***	0.234***	0.060***	0.093***	0.045**	0.093***	0.061***	0.117***	0.048**	0.034**
		(0.000)	(0.000)	(0.004)	(0.000)	(0.044)	(0.000)	(0.000)	(0.000)	(0.039)	(0.048)
Obs.		3136	142,255	3057	142,255	3136	142,255	3136	133,237	3057	3057
Adj. R-sq.		0.130	0.160	0.400	0.097	0.069	0.103	0.097	0,136	0.047	0.124
Year FE		Yes	Yes	Yes	Yes	Yes	Yes	Yes	Yes	Yes	Yes
Firm FE		No	No	Yes	Yes	No	No	No	No	Yes	Yes

All variables are defined in Sect. 5.1.2. Standard errors are clustered by firm. *P*-values of coefficient estimates are reported in parentheses and are based on two-tailed tests. Continuous variables are winsorized at the first and 99th percentiles. *, **, and *** define significance at the 10%, 5%, and 1% levels, respectively. Columns 2, 4, 6, and 8 show the results from Ball et al. (2013), respectively, reported in Table 5, Row 1; Table 5, Row 5; Table 5, Row 3; and Table 4, Row 3

Table 5.3 Information asymmetry and financial leverage as drivers of capital markets' demand for conservatism

		EARN		ΔEARN		Unexp. EARN	
Dependent variable:	Exp. Sign	(1)	(2)	(3)	(4)	(5)	(6)
RET	+	0.069***	0.066***	0.071***	0.069***	0.067***	0.064***
		(0.000)	(0.000)	(0.000)	(0.000)	(0.000)	(0.000)
NEG	+/–	0.008	0.004	0.009	0.005	0.005	0.001
		(0.174)	(0.492)	(0.146)	(0.398)	(0.355)	(0.824)
RET*NEG	+	0.033*	0.018	0.029	0.012	0.011	0.001
		(0.070)	(0.315)	(0.128)	(0.517)	(0.486)	(0.959)
RET*NEG*SIZE	+/–	–0.000	0.010	–0.007	–0.003	–0.007	–0.002
		(0.984)	(0.626)	(0.744)	(0.903)	(0.670)	(0.923)
*RET*NEG*VOLATILITY*	+	*0.052****	*0.045***	*0.051***	*0.044**	*0.051****	*0.047***
		(0.008)	*(0.018)*	*(0.023)*	*(0.050)*	*(0.007)*	*(0.012)*
RET*NEG*M/B	+/–	–0.014	–0.009	–0.008	0.000	–0.008	0.002
		(0.397)	(0.656)	(0.686)	(0.987)	(0.641)	(0.912)
*RET*NEG*LEVERAGE*	+	*0.033**	*0.044****	*0.041***	*0.061****	*0.037***	*0.039***
		(0.055)	*(0.010)*	*(0.048)*	*(0.003)*	*(0.012)*	*(0.011)*
RET*NEG*LAG_EARN	+/–	0.003	–0.015	–0.012	–0.025	0.006	–0.002
		(0.912)	(0.514)	(0.666)	(0.366)	(0.762)	(0.912)
Observations		3136	3057	3136	3057	3136	3057
Adjusted R-squared		0.445	0.495	0.305	0.380	0.136	0.206
Year fixed effects		Yes	Yes	Yes	Yes	Yes	Yes
Firm fixed effects		No	Yes	No	Yes	No	Yes

All variables are defined in Sect. 5.1.2. Standard errors are clustered by firm. *P*-values of coefficient estimates are reported in parentheses and are based on two-tailed tests. All control variables and their interactions with RET and NEG are included but not reported for brevity. Continuous variables are winsorized at the first and 99th percentiles. *, **, and *** define significance at the 10%, 5%, and 1% levels, respectively

Table 5.4 Association between the Khan and Watts (2009) C-Score measure and the asymmetric recognition timeliness of Italian-listed firms

Dependent variable:	Exp. Sign	EARN		ΔEARN		Unexp.EARN	
		(1)	(2)	(3)	(4)	(5)	(6)
RET	+	0.073***	0.090***	0.069**	0.063**	0.084***	0.083***
		(0.001)	(0.000)	(0.010)	(0.046)	(0.000)	(0.001)
NEG	+/−	−0.012	−0.020*	−0.014	−0.016	−0.015*	−0.019**
		(0.260)	(0.050)	(0.202)	(0.176)	(0.093)	(0.041)
RET*NEG	+/−	0.040	−0.103**	−0.113*	−0.108*	−0.119***	−0.156***
		(0.468)	(0.015)	(0.051)	(0.073)	(0.004)	(0.000)
*RET*NEG*CSCORE*	+	*0.158**	*0.229****	*0.276****	*0.249***	*0.301****	*0.312****
		(0.090)	*(0.003)*	*(0.003)*	*(0.011)*	*(0.000)*	*(0.000)*
Observations		1687	1643	1687	1643	1687	1643
Adjusted R-squared		0.143	0.368	0.125	0.069	0.149	0.133
Year fixed effects		Yes	Yes	Yes	Yes	Yes	Yes
Firm fixed effects		No	Yes	No	Yes	No	Yes

All variables are defined in Sect. 5.1.2. Standard errors are clustered by firm. *P*-values of coefficient estimates are reported in parentheses and are based on two-tailed tests. CSCORE and its interaction with RET and NEG are included but not reported for brevity. Continuous variables are winsorized at the first and 99th percentiles *, **, and *** define significance at the 10%, 5%, and 1% levels, respectively

Table 5.5 Association between the Givoly and Hayn (2000) differential skewness measure and the asymmetric recognition timeliness of Italian-listed firms

		EARN		ΔEARN		Unexp. EARN	
Dependent variable:	Exp. Sign	(1)	(2)	(3)	(4)	(5)	(6)
RET	+	0.067***	0.068***	0.054***	0.051***	0.056***	0.058***
		(0.002)	(0.000)	(0.002)	(0.007)	(0.002)	(0.002)
NEG	+/−	0.013	−0.002	0.005	−0.007	0.005	−0.005
		(0.347)	(0.826)	(0.608)	(0.565)	(0.591)	(0.616)
RET*NEG	+/−	0.042	−0.058	−0.026	−0.061	−0.006	−0.048
		(0.402)	(0.190)	(0.522)	(0.122)	(0.871)	(0.204)
*RET*NEG*ΔSKEWNESS*	+	*0.160***	*0.141**	*0.128**	*0.160***	*0.126***	*0.130***
		(0.029)	*(0.060)*	*(0.069)*	*(0.025)*	*(0.036)*	*(0.045)*
Observations		1537	1485	1537	1485	1537	1485
Adjusted R-squared		0.161	0.443	0.153	0.130	0.174	0.209
Year fixed effects		Yes	Yes	Yes	Yes	Yes	Yes
Firm fixed effects		No	Yes	No	Yes	No	Yes

All variables are defined in Sect. 5.1.2. Standard errors are clustered by firm. *P*-values of coefficient estimates are reported in parentheses and are based on two-tailed tests. ΔSKEWNESS and its interaction with RET and NEG are included but not reported for brevity. Continuous variables are winsorized at the first and 99th percentiles. *, **, and *** define significance at the 10%, 5%, and 1% levels, respectively

Table 5.6 Association between past average negative accruals and the asymmetric recognition timeliness of Italian-listed firms

		EARN		ΔEARN		Unexp.EARN	
Dependent variable:	Exp. Sign	(1)	(2)	(3)	(4)	(5)	(6)
RET	+	0.092***	0.087***	0.089***	0.083***	0.090***	0.082***
		(0.000)	(0.000)	(0.000)	(0.000)	(0.000)	(0.000)
NEG	+/–	0.015	0.019*	0.019*	0.017	0.016*	0.014
		(0.215)	(0.077)	(0.063)	(0.128)	(0.075)	(0.150)
RET*NEG	+/–	0.086*	0.038	0.012	0.012	0.025	0.013
		(0.059)	(0.334)	(0.755)	(0.765)	(0.496)	(0.726)
*RET*NEG*Avg.Neg.Accr.*	+/–	*0.048*	*0.007*	*0.051*	*0.043*	*0.045*	*0.017*
		(0.524)	*(0.915)*	*(0.429)*	*(0.556)*	*(0.466)*	*(0.794)*
Observations		2154	2092	2154	2092	2154	2092
Adjusted R-squared		0.131	0.408	0.118	0.070	0.141	0.163
Year fixed effects		Yes	Yes	Yes	Yes	Yes	Yes
Firm fixed effects		No	Yes	No	Yes	No	Yes

All variables are defined in Sect. 5.1.2. Standard errors are clustered by firm. *P*-values of coefficient estimates are reported in parentheses and are based on two-tailed tests. Avg.Neg.Accr. and its interaction with RET and NEG are included but not reported for brevity. Continuous variables are winsorized at the first and 99th percentiles. *, **, and *** define significance at the 10%, 5%, and 1% levels, respectively possibly indicating its linkage with distinct and conflicting manifestations of conservatism, namely the conditional and unconditional form.

Overall, the study's findings robustly support the use of the Basu (1997) asymmetric timeliness model, modified as in Badia et al. (2021) and Ball et al. (2013), to measure conditional conservatism among firms listed in the Italian stock market. Specifically, the estimation results from Table 5.2 closely mirror those reported by Ball et al. (2013), indicating that the Basu (1997) model captures similar aspects of conservatism across both Italian and U.S. settings, notwithstanding institutional and economic differences. Moreover, the results presented in Table 5.3 reveal that, akin to empirical findings in the U.S. and international contexts, Italian capital market forces significantly influence firms' conditionally conservative accounting practices.

Assessing conditional conservatism at the firm-year level holds paramount importance, particularly when conservatism serves as the independent construct in a researcher's model—such as in investigations into its effects on various market phenomena. Despite the empirical literature's struggle to identify reliable measures, two proxies have emerged as commonly adopted: the Khan and Watts (2009) C-Score and the Givoly and Hayn (2000) differential skewness measure. The results reported in Tables 5.4 and 5.5 lend considerable robustness to using either of these measures, assuaging concerns among researchers studying conservatism's implications in the Italian setting.

5.2 Conservatism's Information Benefits for the Italian Stock Market During the Covid Crisis

5.2.1 Motivation

The onset of the Covid pandemic ushered in a period of unprecedented uncertainty for investors, particularly concerning firms' future prospects. What had previously been deemed sound business models were now cast into doubt. Similarly, once-sustainable revenue streams from contracts with customers may now be questioned (Acunzo et al., 2020). With assets' cash-generating capabilities potentially diminishing, the looming threat of impairment losses and write-downs of uncertain magnitude became a pressing issue (Doni & Liberatore, 2021; Quagli et al., 2021; Braga & Miglietta, 2021).[1] This concern was especially pronounced for companies that had previously employed aggressive accounting practices, inflating the value of their assets to unsustainable levels prior to an economic downturn. Consequently, this environment gave rise to profound uncertainty and disagreement among investors regarding firm valuations. Excessive volatility from tumultuous markets poses

[1] The unprecedented level of uncertainty caused by the pandemic's disruption of the economic activity arguably made it even harder for firms to produce reliable estimates of uncertain losses, such as impairments and write-downs (Quagli et al., 2021; Doni & Liberatore, 2021).

valuation challenges, calling for modified information input usage in the valuation process (Mazzi, 2021). Moreover, unlike past crises, the Covid pandemic was not instigated by economic or social forces but rather by an external factor—the spread of a new lethal virus. This, in turn, led to considerable uncertainty regarding the anticipated duration of the crisis (Giorgio & Carnazza, 2020).

Against this backdrop, the second study presented in this chapter delves into the behavior of the Italian stock market amid the unraveling Covid crisis. Specifically, it seeks to explore the role of conservatism in assuaging investor uncertainty, potentially leading to less negative stock price performance, reduced volatility, and diminished investor disagreement. Several theoretical considerations suggest that conservatism could play a pivotal role in this context. Firstly, firms adhering to high levels of conservatism are less inclined to overstate asset values relative to their economic fundamentals. By mandating the prompt recognition of adverse economic events in financial statements, conservatism provides investors with reassurance regarding the absence of concealed losses of unforeseeable magnitude that might suddenly emerge during crises (i.e., the "tip of the iceberg" effect). Additionally, stricter verification standards for recognizing revenue help ensure that valuations based on future revenue projections are not as vulnerable to concerns of sudden revenue loss if economic conditions worsen. Moreover, less-conservative firms are more likely to engage in inefficient investments (Garcìa Lara et al., 2016) that could negatively affect performance in the wake of a crisis.

Existing literature, predominantly focused on the U.S. context, has revealed that conservatism can enhance the information environment by mitigating information asymmetry, reducing market uncertainty, and minimizing investor disagreement (D'Augusta et al., 2016; Garcìa Lara et al., 2014; LaFond & Watts, 2008). International studies indicate that conservatism's information benefits may have played a crucial role amidst the significant valuation uncertainties triggered by the unfolding pandemic. For instance, Cui et al. (2021) found that among Chinese firms listed on the Shanghai and Shenzhen Stock Exchanges, those that adopted more conservative reporting practices experienced less pronounced declines in stock returns compared to their peers. Similarly, D'Augusta and Grossetti (2023) showed that conservatism facilitated investors' interpretation of earnings news in early 2020, reducing return volatility. These findings are consistent with earlier evidence of conservatism's benefits during the 2008 financial crisis in the U.S. market (Balakrishnan et al., 2016).

In contrast to the aforementioned research, this study examines the response of the Italian stock market to the Covid crisis. Analyzing the Italian context offers valuable empirical insights for several reasons. As Mattei et al. (2023) highlighted, Italy was the first country outside China to be significantly impacted by the pandemic, signaling to global markets that the outbreak could not be contained. Moreover, the Italian government was among the most active in implementing emergency measures in response to the crisis (Buchetti et al., 2022). Consistently, Mauro et al. (2023) showed a significant negative stock market reaction following the announcement of the first Covid case in Italy, with a downward trend continuing through the national lockdown and then followed by a reversal as government intervention by the Italian government and E.U. institutions was rolling out. Interestingly, both Carletti et al. (2020) and Mauro et al. (2023) revealed that performance during the pandemic varied across Italian companies, depending on firm-specific characteristics such as public versus private ownership or pre-Covid leverage ratios.

These findings prompt the question of whether conservatism significantly influenced the stock performance of Italian firms during the Covid crisis. Surprisingly, such effects have been scarcely investigated. Furthermore, the broader inquiry into whether conservatism plays a beneficial informational role in the Italian stock market has not received adequate empirical attention compared to the extensive evidence from international studies.

To address this gap, this study examines the stock performance of Italian firms in the weeks preceding and following the announcement of the national lockdown by the Italian government on March ninth, 2020. The results shed light on the significant impact of a firm's level of conservatism in pre-Covid financial statements on various stock market outcomes, including cumulative abnormal returns, daily return volatility, and abnormal trade patterns. Consistent with expectations drawn from evidence in the U.S. market, the empirical findings presented in this study contribute to our understanding of conservatism's implications for stock market dynamics across different institutional contexts within the international accounting landscape.

5.2.2 *Research Design*

I conduct three sets of empirical tests to study the stock market effect of conservatism during the Covid crisis. The first set examines the association between conservatism and the cumulative abnormal return (CAR) over the 45, 60, and 90 trading days beginning on the day of the national lockdown announcement (i.e., day zero: March 9th, 2020). These three variables are labeled CAR(0,+45), CAR(0,+60), and CAR(0,+90). Abnormal returns are computed by subtracting the value-weighted average market return from stock returns. Conservatism is measured using the Khan and Watts (2009) C-Score proxy (CSCORE) running annual regressions of the Basu (1997) as modified by Ball et al. (2013). The test is conducted utilizing the following regression equation:

$$\text{CAR}(0,+45),\text{CAR}(0,+60),\text{CAR}(0,+90) = \beta 0 + \beta 1\text{CSCORE} + \text{CONTROLS} + \varepsilon \quad (5.4)$$

The equation above focuses on coefficient β1, which is predicted to be positive if conservatism improves stock price performance during the Covid crisis. CONTROLS represents a vector of covariates such as the logarithm of the market value of equity

(SIZE), the leverage ratio calculated as total liabilities divided by total assets (LEVERAGE), the market-to-book ratio (M/B), the level (EARN) and year-over-year change (ΔEARN) of earnings before extraordinary items scaled by the beginning-of-the-year market value of equity. All these variables are calculated at the fiscal year's end closing in 2019.[2] The control variables also include the standard deviation of earnings (EARN_VOL) and cash flows (CFO_VOL), scaled by the market value of equity, over a rolling window of up to 5 years before the fiscal year closing during 2019. Finally, to account for heterogeneity in stock liquidity and volatility, the control variable vector includes the standard deviation of daily returns over the calendar year 2019 (VOLATILITY) and the average trade volume scaled by total shares outstanding over the 90 days before the lockdown announcement (VOLUME).

The second set of tests focuses on stock return differences in the weeks before the lockdown announcement, specifically the ten trading days that separate the first Italian Covid case announcement from the lockdown (days from −10 to −1), the 10 days prior to the first Covid case (from −20 to −11) and the 70 days before (from −90 to −21). The test employs the following regression equation:

$$\begin{aligned}\mathrm{CAR}(-10,-1),\mathrm{CAR}(-20,-11),\mathrm{CAR}(-90,-21) &= \beta 0+\beta 1\mathrm{CSCORE}\\ &+\mathrm{CONTROLS}+\varepsilon\end{aligned} \tag{5.5}$$

The third set of tests focuses on a different aspect of conservatism's valuation consequences and how they affect the stock price response to the Covid crisis. Specifically, the test aims to examine whether conservatism reduces stock market uncertainty and investor disagreement, which is consistent with conservatism playing a beneficial information role in alleviating investor valuation concerns. Consistent with prior literature (D'Augusta & Grossetti, 2023), uncertainty is measured by abnormal return volatility (Abn.VOLATILITY), that is, the difference between daily return volatility over the post-lockdown window (0,+90) and the pre-lockdown window (−90,0). Investor disagreement is similarly measured by abnormal trade volume (Abn.VOLUME), measured as the difference between share turnover over the same pre- and post-lockdown windows used for the calculation of Abn.VOLATILITY. The test is conducted using the following regression equation:

$$\begin{aligned}\mathrm{Abn.VOLATILITY},\mathrm{Abn.VOLUME} &= \beta 0+\beta 1\mathrm{CSCORE}\\ &+\mathrm{CONTROLS}+\varepsilon\end{aligned} \tag{5.6}$$

In the equation above, the coefficient β1 is expected to be negative if conservatism alleviates stock market uncertainty and investor disagreement, resulting in lower return volatility and abnormal trade.

[2] December 2019 for the vast majority of firms, earlier months (e.g., June) for the others.

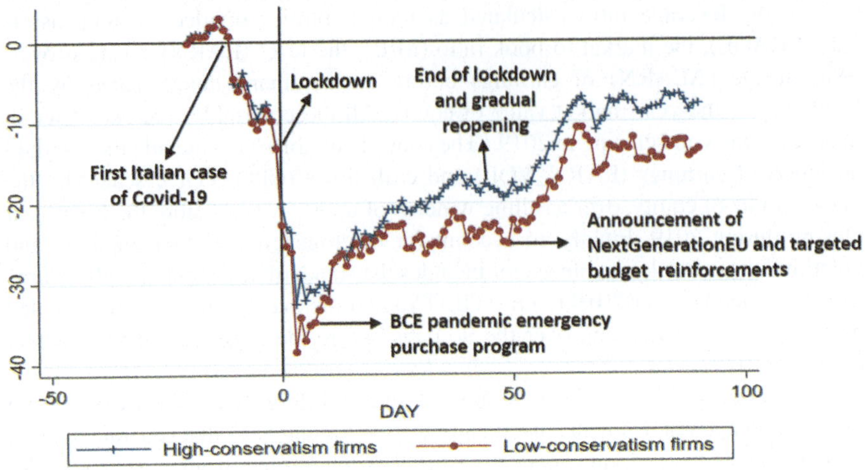

Fig. 5.1 This graph shows the pattern of buy-and-hold returns (Y-axis, expressed in percentage points) during the 20 days before and 90 days after the lockdown announcement (day zero). The values are reported in Table 5.7

5.2.3 Results and Discussion

The sample consists of 159 firm observations for one fiscal year (i.e., the one closing in 2019). The data are obtained from the Compustat Global database through the Wharton Research Data Services website. Before delving into the regression analysis, this section first presents preliminary visual evidence of conservatism's effect on stock market patterns during the pandemic. Fig. 5.1 and Table 5.7 illustrate the value-weighted average buy-and-hold stock return from t-20 to t + 90 for two distinct subsets of firms: high-conservatism and low-conservatism, defined using the median value of CSCORE as the cutoff. In the 2 weeks leading up to the first confirmed case of Covid in Italy, both groups exhibited weakly positive returns, with negligible differences between them. However, the emergence of the pandemic had a severe adverse impact on the Italian stock market, leading to nearly a 13% loss for both sets of firms in the subsequent weeks.

Over the 4 days after the government announced a national lockdown, low-conservatism firms suffered a more substantial decline, experiencing an approximately 25% fall in stock prices. In contrast, high-conservatism firms displayed a comparatively less negative response during the same period, resulting in a noticeable difference of about 6% in cumulative returns between the two groups. This disparity suggests that conservatism may have played a pivotal role in reassuring investors about the valuation consequences of the unfolding crisis. As the crisis persisted, both groups gradually recovered a portion of their losses over the subsequent 2 months. However, high-conservatism firms consistently outperformed their low-conservatism counterparts by approximately 4–6%. This trend aligns with the

Table 5.7 Buy-and-hold returns before and after the lockdown announcement by the Italian government

Day	High conservatism	Low conservatism	Difference	Day	High conservatism	Low conservatism	Difference
−20	0.06%	−0.08%	0.15%	*20*	−24.00%	−24.69%	0.69%
−19	0.86%	0.53%	0.33%	*21*	−23.08%	−23.79%	0.71%
−18	1.06%	0.86%	0.20%	*22*	−22.28%	−24.11%	1.83%
−17	0.91%	0.72%	0.18%	*23*	−20.83%	−22.92%	2.08%
−16	0.88%	0.84%	0.04%	*24*	−20.83%	−22.92%	2.08%
−15	1.57%	1.99%	−0.41%	*25*	−20.83%	−22.92%	2.08%
−14	2.00%	1.98%	0.02%	*26*	−19.76%	−22.61%	2.84%
−13	2.95%	3.02%	−0.07%	*27*	−21.00%	−25.66%	4.65%
−12	1.66%	1.62%	0.04%	*28*	−21.17%	−25.64%	4.47%
−11	0.59%	0.80%	−0.21%	*29*	−20.61%	−24.53%	3.92%
−10	−5.10%	−4.48%	−0.62%	*30*	−19.94%	−24.11%	4.18%
−9	−5.41%	−6.03%	0.62%	*31*	−20.76%	−26.34%	5.58%
−8	−3.79%	−4.76%	0.98%	*32*	−19.51%	−25.36%	5.85%
−7	−5.31%	−6.60%	1.29%	*33*	−19.62%	−25.01%	5.39%
−6	−7.82%	−9.99%	2.17%	*34*	−19.28%	−25.28%	6.00%
−5	−9.51%	−10.83%	1.33%	*35*	−18.28%	−23.63%	5.35%
−4	−8.18%	−9.82%	1.64%	*36*	−17.85%	−22.50%	4.66%
−3	−7.70%	−8.39%	0.68%	*37*	−17.21%	−21.11%	3.90%
−2	−9.60%	−9.80%	0.20%	*38*	−16.64%	−21.96%	5.31%
−1	−13.08%	−13.22%	0.14%	*39*	−16.64%	−21.96%	5.31%
0	−20.08%	−22.71%	2.63%	*40*	−17.99%	−24.70%	6.71%
1	−22.95%	−25.34%	2.38%	*41*	−17.20%	−23.35%	6.15%
2	−23.65%	−26.09%	2.44%	*42*	−18.32%	−24.25%	5.92%
3	−32.61%	−38.50%	5.89%	*43*	−18.83%	−23.63%	4.80%
4	−29.04%	−34.25%	5.21%	*44*	−17.71%	−22.80%	5.09%
5	−32.14%	−37.08%	4.94%	*45*	−18.08%	−23.06%	4.98%
6	−30.75%	−35.20%	4.45%	*46*	−18.43%	−22.61%	4.17%
7	−31.12%	−34.82%	3.70%	*47*	−18.80%	−23.61%	4.81%
8	−30.16%	−33.31%	3.15%	*48*	−19.42%	−24.90%	5.48%
9	−30.21%	−31.81%	1.60%	*49*	−19.01%	−25.05%	6.04%
10	−30.92%	−32.22%	1.29%	*50*	−17.62%	−22.20%	4.58%
11	−27.60%	−27.39%	−0.21%	*51*	−18.62%	−23.52%	4.90%
12	−2.81%	−26.84%	0.02%	*52*	−18.21%	−22.43%	4.22%
13	−25.97%	−26.27%	0.30%	*53*	−18.33%	−22.60%	4.28%
14	−26.75%	−27.83%	1.08%	*54*	−17.52%	−22.07%	4.55%
15	−25.48%	−26.44%	0.96%	*55*	−15.82%	−20.45%	4.63%
16	−23.37%	−25.01%	1.64%	*60*	−11.38%	−17.09%	5.70%
17	−25.17%	−26.53%	1.37%	*70*	−9.48%	−15.58%	6.10%
18	−23.87%	−24.47%	0.60%	*80*	−8.26%	−13.96%	5.70%
19	−24.31%	−25.96%	1.65%	*90*	−7.81%	−13.46%	5.65%

Table 5.8 Descriptive statistics

	Obs.	Mean	Std. Dev.	25th perc.	Median	75th perc.
CAR(−10, −1)	159	−0.0300	0.0918	−0.0891	−0.0338	0.0320
CAR(−20, −11)	159	−0.0269	0.0534	−0.0555	−0.0327	−0.0031
CAR(−90, −21)	159	−0.0125	0.1432	−0.0946	−0.0241	0.0591
CSCORE	159	0.0605	0.0908	0.0007	0.0544	0.1239
CAR(0, +45)	159	0.1374	0.1691	0.0161	0.1228	0.2475
CAR(0, +60)	159	0.1345	0.1754	0.0311	0.1244	0.2371
CAR(0, +90)	159	0.0575	0.2013	−0.0784	0.0405	0.1653
Abn. VOLATILITY	159	0.0104	0.0082	0.0066	0.0094	0.0142
Abn. VOLUME	159	0.0087	0.1231	−0.0304	−0.0002	0.0463
SIZE	159	5.6915	1.8428	4.2600	5.3033	7.2107
VOLATILITY	159	0.0185	0.0062	0.0143	0.0171	0.0216
M/B	159	2.5719	2.2210	1.1409	1.8954	2.8983
LEVERAGE	159	0.5961	0.1664	0.4908	0.6123	0.7096
EARN	159	0.0363	0.0865	0.0168	0.0511	0.0800
ΔEARN	159	−0.0138	0.0663	−0.0332	−0.0006	0.0149
EARN_VOL	159	0.0372	0.0351	0.0148	0.0256	0.0464
CFO_VOL	159	0.0645	0.0661	0.0223	0.0384	0.0863
VOLUME	159	0.2007	0.2036	0.0535	0.1370	0.2773

notion that conservatism could enhance a firm's ability to navigate crises, boosting investor confidence and contributing to an expedited stock price recovery.

Overall, the graph provides compelling visual evidence indicating that conservatism likely played a significant role in mitigating the initial negative market response to the crisis and facilitating the subsequent recovery of stock prices.

Next, conservatism's stock market effects during the Covid crisis are formally tested through the multivariate regression equations discussed in the previous section. Table 5.8 shows descriptive statistics for the variables included in the regression models. Table 5.9 reports the results from regression Eq. (5.4). Consistent with expectations, the coefficient of CSCORE is significantly positive in all three event windows, i.e. the 45, 60, and 90 days after the lockdown announcement. In particular, the results suggest that increasing conservatism by one standard deviation corresponds to cumulative abnormal returns of about 6% higher over the window (0, +60), consistent with the average difference between low- and high-conservatism firms reported in Table 5.7.

Table 5.10 reports the results for Eq. (5.5), focusing on the cumulative abnormal returns in the period before the lockdown announcement. The results show that conservatism already played a beneficial effect in the 2 weeks leading to the lockdown (i.e., the window −10,0). This is consistent with the market already pricing the imminent crisis after the announcement of the first Italian Covid case (i.e., day −10) and with conservatism mitigating the expected economic consequences of the

Table 5.9 Effect of conservatism on post-lockdown abnormal returns

Dependent variable:	Exp. Sign	CAR(0,+45) (1)	CAR(0,+60) (2)	CAR(0,+90) (3)
CSCORE	+	*0.043**	*0.064****	*0.058***
		(0.057)	*(0.010)*	*(0.042)*
SIZE	+/−	0.010	0.040*	0.043
		(0.647)	(0.087)	(0.134)
VOLATILITY	+/−	0.023	0.019	0.041
		(0.297)	(0.373)	(0.128)
M/B	+/−	0.038**	0.035**	0.031*
		(0.023)	(0.039)	(0.077)
LEVERAGE	+/−	−0.047***	−0.051**	−0.049**
		(0.009)	(0.011)	(0.039)
EARN	+/−	−0.001	0.006	0.020
		(0.960)	(0.831)	(0.503)
ΔEARN	+/−	−0.002	−0.004	0.002
		(0.938)	(0.851)	(0.948)
EARN_VOL	+/−	0.007	0.006	0.005
		(0.671)	(0.734)	(0.793)
CFO_VOL	+/−	0.016	−0.007	−0.003
		(0.328)	(0.650)	(0.863)
VOLUME	+/−	0.018	0.034	0.016
		(0.392)	(0.131)	(0.566)
Constant	+/−	0.137***	0.134***	0.058***
		(0.000)	(0.000)	(0.000)
Observations		159	159	159
Adjusted R-squared		0.084	0.075	0.045

All variables are defined in Sect. 5.2.2. Standard errors are clustered by firm. *P*-values of coefficient estimates are reported in parentheses and are based on two-tailed tests. Continuous variables are winsorized the first and 99th percentiles. *, **, and *** define significance at the 10%, 5%, and 1% levels, respectively

crisis. However, the effect of conservatism appears insignificant in earlier time windows, consistent with the market not pricing conservatism per se but rather conservatism's effect on the economic consequences of adverse events.

Table 5.11 reports the results for Eq. (5.6), focusing on conservatism's effects on abnormal volatility and abnormal trade volume after the lockdown announcement. In line with expectations, these effects are negative. This suggests that conservatism not only improves stock performance (as per the results displayed in Table 5.9) but also mitigates investor uncertainty and disagreement about the correct valuation of the firm equity.

Finally, Table 5.12 repeats all the tests discussed above using decile-ranks of CSCORE instead of the continuous variable to mitigate outlier concerns. All the results appear robust to this alternative specification.

Table 5.10 Effect of conservatism on pre-lockdown abnormal returns

		CAR(−10,-1)	CAR(−20,-11)	CAR(−90,-21)
Dependent variable:	Exp. Sign	(1)	(2)	(3)
CSCORE	+/−	*0.023***	*0.006*	*0.022*
		(0.038)	*(0.442)*	*(0.308)*
SIZE	+/−	0.020**	0.007	0.015
		(0.045)	(0.259)	(0.451)
VOLATILITY	+/−	−0.013	−0.004	−0.008
		(0.194)	(0.548)	(0.550)
M/B	+/−	0.017**	0.004	0.033***
		(0.026)	(0.467)	(0.007)
LEVERAGE	+/−	−0.019**	−0.001	−0.012
		(0.014)	(0.812)	(0.433)
EARN	+/−	−0.002	−0.000	0.044**
		(0.903)	(0.981)	(0.027)
ΔEARN	+/−	−0.001	0.008	−0.009
		(0.925)	(0.301)	(0.663)
EARN_VOL	+/−	−0.002	−0.005	0.007
		(0.765)	(0.337)	(0.709)
CFO_VOL	+/−	0.012	0.010**	−0.011
		(0.178)	(0.048)	(0.495)
VOLUME	+/−	−0.020**	0.003	0.029
		(0.033)	(0.489)	(0.151)
Constant	+/−	−0.030***	−0.027***	−0.013
		(0.000)	(0.000)	(0.248)
Observations		159	159	159
Adjusted R-squared		0.140	0.009	0.097

All variables are defined in Sect. 5.2.2. Standard errors are clustered by firm. *P*-values of coefficient estimates are reported in parentheses and are based on two-tailed tests. Continuous variables are winsorized at the first and 99th percentiles. *, **, and *** define significance at the 10%, 5%, and 1% levels, respectively

In summary, the results presented in this study shed light on the role of conservatism in shaping stock market responses to the unprecedented challenges posed by the Covid crisis in Italy. The findings suggest that firms characterized by higher levels of conservatism exhibited more resilient stock performance throughout the crisis period, mitigating initial losses and facilitating swifter recoveries. Moreover, the analysis shows that conservatism's effects were not limited to stock returns but also extended to abnormal volatility and trade volume, suggesting its role in mitigating investor uncertainty and disagreement regarding firm valuation.

The evidence indicating that high-conservatism firms experienced less severe declines and achieved better post-crisis stock performance than their low-conservatism counterparts underscores the potential benefits of conservative accounting practices during economic turmoil. This suggests that conservative

Table 5.11 Effect of conservatism on post-lockdown volatility and disagreement

		Abn. VOLATILITY	Abn. VOLUME
Dependent variable:	Exp. Sign	(1)	(2)
CSCORE	–	*−0.002**	*−0.049****
		(0.061)	*(0.004)*
SIZE	+/–	0.000	0.010
		(0.619)	(0.581)
VOLATILITY	+/–	0.001	−0.011
		(0.421)	(0.479)
M/B	+/–	−0.000	−0.003
		(0.815)	(0.789)
LEVERAGE	+/–	0.001	0.026*
		(0.328)	(0.070)
EARN	+/–	−0.003*	−0.036*
		(0.051)	(0.067)
ΔEARN	+/–	0.001	0.020
		(0.666)	(0.279)
EARN_VOL	+/–	−0.001	0.012
		(0.276)	(0.213)
CFO_VOL	+/–	−0.000	−0.015
		(0.778)	(0.143)
VOLUME	+/–	−0.002**	−0.031
		(0.046)	(0.138)
Constant	+/–	0.010***	0.009
		(0.000)	(0.319)
Observations		159	159
Adjusted R-squared		0.090	0.207

All variables are defined in Sect. 5.2.2. Standard errors are clustered by firm. *P*-values of coefficient estimates are reported in parentheses and are based on two-tailed tests. Continuous variables are winsorized at the first and 99th percentiles. *, **, and *** define significance at the 10%, 5%, and 1% levels, respectively

reporting may provide investors with greater clarity and confidence in uncertain times and help firms navigate crises more effectively.

However, it is important to acknowledge the study's limitations, including potential confounding variables and the generalizability of the findings beyond the Italian stock market. Future research could delve deeper into the underlying mechanisms through which conservatism influences stock market dynamics during crises and explore its implications across diverse geographical and institutional settings. Nevertheless, this study contributes valuable insights into the role of conservatism in enhancing firm stock performance resilience and investor confidence amidst unprecedented challenges.

Table 5.12 Robustness test using conservatism decile-ranks

	CAR(0,+45)	CAR(0,+60)	CAR(0,+90)	CAR(−10,-1)	CAR(−20,-11)	CAR(−90,-21)	Abn.VOLATILITY	Abn.VOLUME
Dependent variable:	(1)	(2)	(3)	(4)	(5)	(6)	(7)	(8)
CSCORE.Rank	0.017**	0.023***	0.019*	0.008**	0.001	0.005	−0.001*	−0.018***
	(0.030)	(0.006)	(0.051)	(0.039)	(0.616)	(0.511)	(0.092)	(0.003)
Observations	159	159	159	159	159	159	159	159
Adjusted R-sq.	0.090	0.080	0.043	0.140	0.006	0.092	0.088	0.214

All variables are defined in Sect. 5.2.2. The variable CSCORE.Rank represents the decile ranking of CSCORE. Standard errors are clustered by firm. *P*-values of coefficient estimates are reported in parentheses and are based on two-tailed tests. Control variables are not included for brevity. Continuous variables are winsorized at the first and 99th percentiles. *, **, and *** define significance at the 10%, 5%, and 1% levels, respectively

5.3 Did Italian Public Firms Become Less Conservative during the Post-Covid Recovery?

5.3.1 Motivation

Accounting regulations leave sufficient room for managerial discretion in deciding when to report profits and losses, leading to variations in reporting conservatism across firms (Lawrence et al., 2013). Managers, motivated by personal incentives tied to compensation and job security, may delay recognizing uncertain losses while accelerating the reporting of profits. Such behavior may cause some firms to deviate from adherence to conservative accounting practices. Capital market pressures represent a significant driver of conservatism differences across firms. Conservative reporting offers informational advantages to parties engaged in contracts with the firm, mitigating various agency conflicts. Therefore, lenders' and shareholders' demand for conservative accounting and their ability to enforce such a demand can counteract the managerial tendency to engage in anti-conservative reporting behavior.

Economic crises serve as compelling settings for studying shifts in a firm's conservative reporting, as they profoundly impact both managerial incentives and the demand for conservatism in capital markets. On the one hand, in the aftermath of a crisis, firms have to navigate challenging economic conditions, and those struggling to recover face heightened distress risks (Carletti et al., 2020). This prospect may prompt creditors to tighten credit supplies and shareholders to consider trimming executive pay or exploring managerial changes. Consequently, managers may hesitate to recognize negative performance while being eager to signal early recovery by anticipating profits' recognition, resulting in a decline in conservatism. On the other hand, research suggests that capital market participants become sensitive to increased uncertainty and information asymmetry during crises, wary of the possibility of strategic reporting behavior by managers. Thus, firms facing robust capital market demand for conservatism are less likely to exhibit reduced conservatism in the aftermath of the crisis.

Studies focusing on the Italian context underscore how managerial incentives can drive opportunistic reporting behavior, leading to decreased conservatism. For instance, Cameran and Campa (2012) provided evidence of Italian managers resorting to aggressive reporting to strategically avoid small losses. Similarly, Sorrentino and Roncagliolo (2014, p. 649) highlighted inconsistencies between consolidated and separate reports, "which could hide management opportunistic behaviors that try to avoid goodwill impairment losses." Mattei and Ricciardi (2012) suggested that managers' incentives toward transparent reporting behavior are a crucial predictor of conservatism changes post-IFRS adoption. Additionally, Cameran et al. (2016) argued that Italy's diverse regulatory requirements, including mandatory auditor rotation, present an intriguing case for conservatism studies.

These insights raise concerns about whether Italian firms strategically reduced conservatism levels as they navigated the challenging post-Covid recovery. Evidence suggests that managers of Italian private firms leaned toward non-conservative reporting choices post-pandemic, hesitant to make disclosures that might unfavorably impact their firms' standing in capital markets. For instance, Di Fabio et al. (2023) showed that firms rarely resorted to temporary government-granted exceptions[3] that could trigger creditors' concerns about the firm's ability to stay in business. Similarly, Quagli (2021) argued that Italian private companies mostly preferred to take the opportunity to adopt equity-increasing measures that could strengthen balance sheet ratios. Furthermore, questions arise about whether Italian firms' financial statements accurately reflected the heightened risks and potential liabilities post-crisis, such as those related to debt repayment and employee downsizing (Ponzio & Zennaro, 2021).[4]

Despite these concerns, empirical attention to conservatism patterns exhibited by Italian-listed firms following the Covid crisis remains scarce. Addressing this gap is crucial as it contributes to understanding Italian firms' financial reporting practices in the post-pandemic era and sheds light on whether Italian capital market forces could counteract managerial tendencies toward non-conservative reporting behavior. Importantly, these findings also contribute to understanding how economic crises impact reporting conservatism, an aspect that international or U.S.-focused empirical research has not fully clarified, as discussed in Chap. 4.

5.3.2 Research Design

The sample of this third study consists of 531 firm-year observations for the fiscal years 2019, 2020, 2021, and 2022. The data are obtained from the Compustat Global database through the Wharton Research Data Services website. The POST-COVID variable is set to one for the fiscal years 2021 and 2022 and zero otherwise. The change in conservatism in the post-Covid period is tested through the following specification of the Basu (1997) model:

$$\begin{aligned} \text{EARN}, \Delta\text{EARN} = {} & \beta 0 + \beta 1\text{POST-COVID} + \beta 2\text{RET} \\ & + \beta 3\text{POST-COVID} * \text{RET} + \beta 4\text{NEG} \\ & + \beta 5\text{POST-COVID} * \text{NEG} + \beta 6\text{RET} * \text{NEG} \\ & + \beta 7\text{POST-COVID} * \text{RET} * \text{NEG} + \varepsilon \end{aligned} \tag{5.7}$$

[3] The Italian government introduced several temporary exceptions to the measurement criteria required by national accounting principles (e.g., postponement of depreciation charges, asset revaluation, exceptions related to the going concern principle and the neutralization of losses), whose impact on financial statements raised perplexities (e.g., Quagli, 2020).

[4] These concerns are not limited to the fiscal year 2020, as the ongoing conflict in Eastern Europe, as well as the protracted volatility in the financial markets, has led to a prolonged period of uncertainty as well as emergency countermeasures by the Italian government (Olante & Daniele, 2023).

In the equation above, the dependent variable is either the level (EARN) or the year-over-year change (ΔEARN) in earnings before extraordinary items scaled by the beginning-of-the-year market value of equity. RET is the annual unexpected stock return calculated as in Ball et al. (2013), and NEG is a binary variable identifying negative RET observations. The variable POST-COVID*RET*NEG identifies the change in conservatism after the crisis. Therefore, if conservatism decreases during the post-Covid recovery, β7 is expected to be negative.

The pre-Covid capital market demand for conservatism is measured by the value of the Khan and Watts (2009) C-Score proxy, which estimates the annual level of conservatism driven by capital market factors such as market capitalization, market-to-book ratio, and market leverage. C-Score is computed by running annual regressions of the Basu (1997) model, as modified by Ball et al. (2013) and Badia et al. (2021). To gauge whether the change in conservatism varies depending on the pre-Covid capital market demand for conservatism, the model of Eq. (5.7) is modified by including an additional interaction with the variable HighDemand, which is set to one if the value of C-Score in the fiscal year 2018 is above the median, and zero otherwise. Therefore, the test is conducted using the following regression equation:

$$\begin{aligned}\mathrm{EARN}, \Delta\mathrm{EARN} = {} & \beta 0 + \beta 1\mathrm{POST} - \mathrm{COVID} + \beta 2\mathrm{RET} \\ & + \beta 3\mathrm{POST} - \mathrm{COVID} * \mathrm{RET} + \beta 4\mathrm{NEG} \\ & + \beta 5\mathrm{POST} - \mathrm{COVID} * \mathrm{NEG} + \beta 6\mathrm{RET} * \mathrm{NEG} \\ & + \beta 7\mathrm{POST} - \mathrm{COVID} * \mathrm{RET} * \mathrm{NEG} + \beta 8\mathrm{HighDemand} \\ & + \beta 9\mathrm{HighDemand} * \mathrm{POST} - \mathrm{COVID} \\ & + \beta 10\mathrm{HighDemand} * \mathrm{RET} + \beta 11\mathrm{HighDemand} * \mathrm{POST} \\ & - \mathrm{COVID} * \mathrm{RET} + \beta 12\mathrm{HighDemand} * \mathrm{NEG} \\ & + \beta 13\mathrm{HighDemand} * \mathrm{POST} - \mathrm{COVID} * \mathrm{NEG} \\ & + \beta 14\mathrm{HighDemand} * \mathrm{RET} * \mathrm{NEG} \\ & + \beta 15\mathrm{HighDemand} * \mathrm{POST} - \mathrm{COVID} * \mathrm{RET} * \mathrm{NEG} \\ & + \mathrm{CONTROLS} + \varepsilon \end{aligned} \tag{5.8}$$

If conservatism decreased during the post-Covid recovery for firms exposed to weak capital market demand for conservatism but did not decrease (or did so to a lesser extent) for firms facing strong demand, β7 is expected to be negative, but β15 is expected to be positive.

In Eq. (5.8), the CONTROLS vector comprises variables such as the logarithm of the market value of equity (SIZE), the market-to-book ratio (M/B), the leverage ratio calculated as total liabilities divided by total assets (LEVERAGE), daily stock return volatility (VOLATILITY), and the prior year value of EARN (LAG_EARN), with their interactions with RET, NEG, and RET*NEG, following the standard approach in the conservatism literature. Table 5.13 reports the descriptive statistics.

Table 5.13 Descriptive statistics

	Obs.	Mean	Std. Dev.	25th perc.	Median	75th perc.
RET	522	0.0216	0.4149	−0.2444	−0.0580	0.1842
EARN	522	0.0409	0.0964	0.0153	0.0488	0.0810
ΔEARN	522	0.0150	0.1501	−0.0263	0.0031	0.0310
CFO	521	0.1722	0.2427	0.0555	0.1166	0.2172
SIZE	522	5.8717	1.9507	4.4746	5.6411	7.3811
VOLATILITY	522	0.0223	0.0078	0.0168	0.0212	0.0265
M/B	522	2.5767	2.6418	1.0880	1.8096	2.8332
LEVERAGE	522	0.6069	0.1679	0.4998	0.6288	0.7306
LAG_EARN	522	0.0295	0.1025	0.0164	0.0451	0.0745

All variables are defined in Sect. 5.3.2

5.3.3 *Results and Discussion*

The results for the regression of Eq. (5.8) are reported in Table 5.14. First, the results obtained using earnings levels as the dependent variable are presented. In Column 1, the coefficient of POST-COVID*RET*NEG is significantly negative. This suggests that conservatism declined significantly in the aftermath of the crisis for firms not exposed to a strong capital market demand for conservative reporting. However, the coefficient of HighDemand*POST-COVID*RET*NEG is of the opposite sign and statistically significant at less than the 5% level. This shows that, in contrast to the prior set of firms, those subject to a stronger capital market demand for conservatism did not report more aggressively. These results support the notion that capital markets' forces can pressure firms into reporting conservatively, thus mitigating managers' strategic tendency to engage in aggressive accounting practices during economic downturns.

Column 2 of Table 5.14 reports the results obtained after interacting with the variable HighDemand all covariates, including the control variables. Columns 3 and 4 report the results using the year-over-year change in earnings as the dependent variable instead of earnings levels. In all three cases, the results are consistent with those presented in Column 1.

Table 5.15 presents the results after substituting the dependent variable with operating cash flow. Collins et al. (2014) showed that conservatism estimates derived from the Basu (1997) model can be affected by cash flow asymmetry, i.e. the tendency of operating cash flows to be asymmetrically associated with contemporaneous stock returns. Collins et al. (2014) noted that this type of asymmetry is unlikely driven by conservatism, which is implemented in the income statements through accruals rather than cash flows, and is likely the source of noise and bias in the Basu (1997) model. Therefore, repeating the test of Eq. 5.8 using operating cash flow as the dependent variable provides a "placebo" test where the coefficients β7

Table 5.14 Association between capital markets' demand for conservatism and asymmetric earnings timeliness after Covid-19

Dependent variable:	Exp. Sign	EARN (1)	EARN (2)	ΔEARN (3)	ΔEARN (4)
RET	+/–	–0.057	–0.076*	–0.055	–0.125*
		(0.106)	(0.071)	(0.310)	(0.067)
NEG	+/–	–0.036	–0.028	–0.027	–0.019
		(0.245)	(0.379)	(0.484)	(0.642)
RET*NEG	+/–	0.180***	0.274***	0.255***	0.538***
		(0.003)	(0.000)	(0.010)	(0.000)
POST-COVID	+/–	–0.042**	–0.039	–0.058**	–0.067**
		(0.047)	(0.104)	(0.040)	(0.028)
POST-COVID*RET	+/–	0.081**	0.097*	0.132*	0.194**
		(0.042)	(0.060)	(0.073)	(0.013)
POST-COVID*NEG	+/–	0.039	0.034	0.035	0.039
		(0.245)	(0.320)	(0.334)	(0.384)
*POST-COVID*RET*NEG*	–	*–0.200**	*–0.212***	*–0.324***	*–0.386***
		(0.070)	*(0.042)*	*(0.023)*	*(0.019)*
*HighDemand*POST-COVID*RET*NEG*	+	*0.305***	*0.377****	*0.324**	*0.516****
		(0.027)	*(0.008)*	*(0.100)*	*(0.009)*
Observations		522	522	522	522
Adjusted R-squared		0.548	0.551	0.654	0.727
CONTROLS		Yes	Yes	Yes	Yes
CONTROLS interactions		Yes	Yes	Yes	Yes
CONTROLS*HighDemand interactions		No	Yes	No	Yes

All variables are defined in Sect. 5.3.2. Standard errors are clustered by firm. *P*-values of coefficient estimates are reported in parentheses and are based on two-tailed tests. All control variables and their interactions are included but not reported for brevity. All models include firm fixed effects. Continuous variables are winsorized at the first and 99th percentiles. *, **, and *** define significance at the 10%, 5%, and 1% levels, respectively

and β15 are expected to be insignificant, thus showing that the results of Table 5.14 are indeed due to changes in conservatism rather than cash flow-related dynamics. Indeed, the results of Table 5.15 show that this is the case: neither POST-COVID*RET*NEG nor HighDemand*POST-COVID*RET*NEG is ever significant, regardless of the model specification.

In conclusion, the regression analysis results, as detailed in Table 5.14, provide compelling evidence regarding the impact of capital market forces on conservatism in the Italian stock market in the aftermath of the Covid crisis. Specifically, the results show a significant decline in conservatism for firms not subject to strong capital market demand for conservative reporting. In contrast, those facing higher demand did not engage in more aggressive accounting practices.

Table 5.15 Placebo test: Association between capital markets' demand for conservatism and asymmetric cash flow timeliness after Covid-19

Dependent variable:	Exp. Sign	CFO (1)	CFO (2)
RET	+/−	−0.117	−0.187
		(0.190)	(0.112)
NEG	+/−	−0.158***	−0.199***
		(0.007)	(0.002)
RET*NEG	+/−	0.316**	0.229*
		(0.022)	(0.088)
POST-COVID	+/−	−0.076	−0.071
		(0.122)	(0.155)
POST-COVID*RET	+/−	0.288*	0.308*
		(0.056)	(0.056)
POST-COVID*NEG	+/−	0.063	0.094
		(0.507)	(0.315)
*POST-COVID*RET*NEG*	+/−	*−0.424*	*−0.430*
		(0.147)	*(0.182)*
*HighDemand*POST-COVID*RET*NEG*	+/−	*0.455*	*0.463*
		(0.302)	*(0.263)*
Observations		521	521
Adjusted R-squared		0.515	0.537
CONTROLS		Yes	Yes
CONTROLS interactions		Yes	Yes
CONTROLS*HighDemand interactions		No	Yes

All variables are defined in Sect. 5.3.2. Standard errors are clustered by firm. *P*-values of coefficient estimates are reported in parentheses and are based on two-tailed tests. All control variables and their interactions are included but not reported for brevity. All models include firm fixed effects. Continuous variables are winsorized at the first and 99th percentiles. *, **, and *** define significance at the 10%, 5%, and 1% levels, respectively

References

Acunzo, G. A., Abate, E., & Amaturo, B. (2020). Covid-19 e l'informativa di semestrale—risultati di un'analisi empirica. *Rivista dei Dottori Commercialisti, 4*, 537–548.

Badia, M., Duro, M., Penalva, F., & Ryan, S. G. (2021). Debiasing the measurement of conditional conservatism. *Journal of Accounting Research, 59*(4), 1221–1259.

Balakrishnan, K., Watts, R. L., & Zuo, L. (2016). The effect of accounting conservatism on corporate investment during the global financial crisis. *Journal of Business Finance & Accounting, 43*(5 & 6), 513–542.

Ball, R., Kothari, S. P., & Nikolaev, V. (2013). On estimating conditional conservatism. *The Accounting Review, 88*(3), 755–787.

Basu, S. (1997). The conservatism principle and the asymmetric timeliness of earnings. *Journal of Accounting and Economics, 24*(1), 3–37.

Braga, L., & Miglietta, S. (2021). L'impairment test dell'avviamento tra IAS 36 e COVID-19. *Bilancio e Revisione, 2*, 13–21.

Buchetti, B., Parbonetti, A., & Pugliese, A. (2022). Covid-19, corporate survival and public policy: The role of accounting information and regulation in the wake of a systemic crisis. *Journal of Accounting and Public Policy, 41*(1), 106919.

Cameran, M., & Campa, D. (2012). La Qualita' del Reddito Migliora Con l'Adozione Degli IAS/IFRS? Il Caso Delle Societa' Italiane Non Quotate. *Rivista dei Dottori Commercialisti*, 275–293. http://www.rivistadeidottoricommercialisti.it/la-qualitÀ-del-reddito-migliora-con-l-adozione-degli-ias-ifrs-il-caso-delle-societÀ-italiane-non-quotate/n-2-aprile-giugno-2012/archivio/128/

Cameran, M., Prencipe, A., & Trombetta, M. (2016). Mandatory audit firm rotation and audit quality. *European Accounting Review, 25*(1), 35–58.

Carletti, E., Oliviero, T., Pagano, M., Pelizzon, L., & Subrahmanyam, M. G. (2020). The COVID-19 shock and equity shortfall: Firm-level evidence from Italy. *The Review of Corporate Finance Studies, 9*(3), 534–568.

Collins, D. W., Hribar, P., & Tian, X. (2014). Cash flow asymmetry: Causes and implications for conditional conservatism research. *Journal of Accounting and Economics, 58*(2–3), 173–200.

Cui, L., Kent, P., Kim, S., & Li, S. (2021). Accounting conservatism and firm performance during the COVID-19 pandemic. *Accounting & Finance, 61*(4), 5543–5579.

D'Augusta, C., Bar-Yosef, S., & Prencipe, A. (2016). The effects of conservative reporting on investor disagreement. *European Accounting Review, 25*(3), 451–485.

D'Augusta, C., & Grossetti, F. (2023). How did Covid-19 affect investors' interpretation of earnings news? The role of accounting conservatism. *Finance Research Letters, 52*, 103504.

Di Fabio, C., Roncagliolo, E., & Simoni, L. (2023). Le deroghe contabili nel contesto dell'emergenza COVID-19: Prime evidenze empiriche. *Rivista dei Dottori Commercialisti, 1*, 1–21.

Dietrich, J. R., Muller, K. A., & Riedl, E. J. (2007). Asymmetric timeliness tests of accounting conservatism. *Review of Accounting Studies, 12*(1), 95–124.

Doni, F., & Liberatore, G. (2021). Il processo di impairment test post Covid-19: Informativa e pratiche valutative nei bilanci 2020. Un'analisi preliminare. *Rivista dei Dottori Commercialisti*, 381–411.

Garcìa Lara, J. M., Garcìa Osma, B., & Penalva, F. (2014). Information consequences of accounting conservatism. *European Accounting Review, 23*(2), 173–198.

Garcìa Lara, J. M., Garcìa Osma, B., & Penalva, F. (2016). Accounting conservatism and firm investment efficiency. *Journal of Accounting and Economics, 61*(1), 221–238.

Giorgio, F., & Carnazza, P. (2020). Gli effetti del COVID - 19 sull'economia italiana e sul sistema produttivo. *Argomenti, 16*, 16.

Givoly, D., & Hayn, C. (2000). The changing time-series properties of earnings, cash flows and accruals: Has financial reporting become more conservative? *Journal of Accounting and Economics, 29*(3), 287–320.

Givoly, D., Hayn, C., & Natarajan, A. (2007). Measuring reporting conservatism. *The Accounting Review, 82*(1), 65–106.

Khan, M., & Watts, R. L. (2009). Estimation and empirical properties of a firm-year measure of accounting conservatism. *Journal of Accounting and Economics, 48*(2–3), 132–150.

LaFond, R., & Watts, R. L. (2008). The information role of conservatism. *The Accounting Review, 83*(2), 447–478.

Lawrence, A., Sloan, R., & Sun, Y. (2013). Non-discretionary conservatism: Evidence and implications. *Journal of Accounting & Economics, 56*, 112–133.

Mattei, M. M., & Ricciardi, M. (2012). Il Principio di Prudenza Dopo l'Adozione degli IAS/IFRS: Un'Analisi Empirica. *Rivista dei Dottori Commercialisti, 1*, 37–62.

Mattei, M. M., Merlo, M., & Monaco, E. (2023). The Italian depreciation suspension policy during the COVID-19 pandemic: Consequences on private firms' borrowing capacity. *Accounting in Europe, 20*(2), 166–193.

Mauro, M., Giancotti, M., Pipitone, V., & Tiscini, R. (2023). Covid-19 on stock market performance: Evidence from Italy. *Economic Research-Ekonomska Istraživanja, 36*(3), 2264369.

Mazzi, F. (2021). Valutazione d'azienda durante la pandemia: Analisi fondamentali ed incorporazione dell'incertezza nei flussi di risultato attesi. *Rivista dei Dottori Commercialisti, 2*, 223–235.

Olante, M. E., & Daniele, M. (2023). Fine del periodo emergenziale: impatti contabili delle misure di sostegno connesse al COVID-19. *Bilancio e Revisione, n., 7*, 21–30.

Patatoukas, P. N., & Thomas, J. K. (2011). More evidence of bias in the differential timeliness measure of conditional conservatism. *The Accounting Review, 86*(5), 1765–1793.

Ponzio, A., & Zennaro, D. (2021). Debiti e fondi per rischi e oneri: misureranno in modo appropriato i rischi da COVID-19? *Bilancio e Revisione, 1*, 55–64.

Quagli, A., Ramassa, P., & Venuti, M. (2021). COVID-19: The impact on IFRS financial reporting. *Financial Reporting, 2*, 161–173.

Quagli, A. (2021). *Deroghe contabili emergenziali: le imprese hanno scelto secondo convenienza*. IPSOA Quotidiano. https://www.ipsoa.it/documents/quotidiano/2022/03/19/deroghe-contabili-emergenziali-imprese-scelto-secondo-convenienza

Quagli, A. (2020). *Covid e normativa emergenziale di bilancio: virata di rotta del Legislatore*. IPSOA Quotidiano. https://www.ipsoa.it/documents/quotidiano/2020/11/14/covid-normativa-emergenziale-bilancio-virata-rotta-legislatore

Sorrentino, M., & Roncagliolo, E. (2014). Un Confronto Sulle Svalutazioni Dell'avviamento Per Impairment Tra Bilancio Consolidato E Bilancio Separato. *Rivista dei Dottori Commercialisti, 4*, 649–671.

Chapter 6
Concluding Remarks

Over the past three decades, researchers have devoted substantial effort to studying accounting conservatism and its relationship with the business environment. A growing body of literature has delved into how conservatism interacts with the stock market, which was relatively unexplored at the beginning of the twenty-first century but has since garnered significant attention. This surge of interest has unveiled a complex picture: while stock market forces can influence conservatism, conservatism, in turn, can have profound economic implications for equity investors. Yet, as is typical in academic research, each discovery raises new questions, paving the way for future exploration.

Private firms offer a compelling frontier for further investigation. In a recent survey of the literature on accounting in private firms, Bar-Yosef et al. (2019) report that the vast majority of the literature examining conservatism in private firms has focused on its determinants rather than consequences. Exploring whether conservatism yields positive or negative effects for private enterprises and how these effects compare to those observed in publicly traded firms presents an intriguing venue for future research, especially in countries like Italy, where privately owned businesses and small to medium enterprises dominate the economic landscape.

Another emerging research stream examines the relationship between conservatism and corporate social responsibility (CSR). Among recent contributions, Anagnostopoulou et al. (2020) showed that conservatism is negatively associated with the firm's CSR orientation. Also, Burke et al. (2020) found that the demand for conservatism is lower for better-performing CSR firms, and Cho et al. (2020) found that conservative firms are less likely to disclose CSR information. As societal concerns regarding social responsibility and sustainability reporting gain prominence, investigating their intersection with conservatism becomes increasingly pertinent.

In international accounting research, an intriguing direction involves exploring the influence of culture on conservative reporting choices. Future studies could, for instance, investigate whether national culture can explain cross-country variation in conservatism in a way similar to what has been done concerning corporate

C. D'Augusta, *Accounting Conservatism and the Stock Market*, SpringerBriefs in Accounting, https://doi.org/10.1007/978-3-031-67145-6_6

governance (Duong et al., 2016). A recent paper examining the relationship between cultural dimensions and conservatism is Zeghal and Lahmar (2018). They found evidence of the impact of culture on conservatism during the transition to international standards in the European Union.

Moreover, the predominance of U.S.-focused empirical analysis in the research discussed in this book underscores the need to examine diverse regulatory, institutional, and cultural contexts. The empirical studies in Chap. 5 shed light on unanswered questions within the Italian setting, revealing the resilience of established conservatism models and showcasing the influence of capital market forces. Despite these insights, the Italian setting presents the opportunity to pursue many additional research venues. As discussed by the end of Chap. 4, significant efforts have been made to understand the relationship between voluntary disclosures and mandatory financial statements in the U.S. context. To what extent do those findings apply to Italy? Does conservatism indirectly influence soft or narrative disclosures? Another line of inquiry concerns aspects related to government intervention, family ownership, and different roles played by lenders in the firm's governance structure, which may have profound implications for the theoretical predictions and empirical manifestations of conservatism in accounting.

In conclusion, while scholars have made considerable advancements in understanding conservatism, ample opportunities exist for further exploration. Future research holds the potential to expand our comprehension of conservatism's economic determinants, consequences, and interactions, thereby enriching our understanding of its role in shaping the business environment.

References

Anagnostopoulou, S. C., Tsekrekos, A. E., & Voulgaris, G. (2020). Accounting conservatism and corporate social responsibility. *British Accounting Review, 53*(4), 100942.

Bar-Yosef, S., D'Augusta, C., & Prencipe, A. (2019). Accounting research in private firms: State of the art and future directions. *The International Journal of Accounting, 54*(02), 1–81.

Burke, Q. L., Chen, P. C., & Lobo, G. J. (2020). Is corporate social responsibility performance related to conditional accounting conservatism? *Accounting Horizons, 34*(2), 19–40.

Cho, S. Y., Kang, P. K., Lee, C., & Park, C. (2020). Financial reporting conservatism and voluntary CSR disclosure. *Accounting Horizons, 34*(2), 63–82.

Duong, H. K., Kang, H., & Salter, S. B. (2016). National culture and corporate governance. *Journal of International Accounting Research, 15*(3), 67–96.

Zeghal, D., & Lahmar, Z. (2018). The effect of culture on accounting conservatism during adoption of IFRS in the EU. *International Journal of Accounting and Information Management, 26*(2), 311–330.

The manufacturer's authorised representative in the EU is Springer
Nature Customer Service Centre GmbH, Europaplatz 3, 69115 Heidelberg,
Germany. If you have any concerns regarding our products, please
contact ProductSafety@springernature.com

Printed and bound by CPI Group (UK) Ltd, Croydon, CR0 4YY
01/10/2026
02225880-0005